INTO THE SAUCE!

* *

From Our Cucina to Your Kitchen

* *

100% Authentic Southern Italian Recipes from

INTO THE SAUCE!

BUCA di BEPPO

Food photography:
E.J. Armstrong, Seattle
Design and typesetting:
Alicia Nammacher
Editor: Shannon O'Leary
Food styling: Diana Isaiou
Recipe testing: Susan Volland
Copy editor and indexer: Miriam Bulmer

TIGER OAK PUBLICATIONS

Custom Publishing Services provided by
Tiger Oak Publications
251 First Avenue North, Suite 401
Minneapolis, Minnesota 55401
(612)338-4125 www.tigeroak.com
ISBN 0-9721029-0-6

PHIL ROBERTS

My thanks ✻ ✻ ✻ Without Phil Roberts there would be no "Buca di Beppo" as we know it today. No half-pound meatballs. No Pope's Table. No Buca Bianco. ✻ ✻ ✻ Buca Little Italy, as the first restaurant in downtown Minneapolis was originally known, was the brainchild of Phil Roberts. This book is a tribute to his vision of what a little "buca" could and should be. ✻ ✻ ✻ Let me tell you about our founder and my partner. I would describe Phil, who is not Italian, as an Italian lover. (Phil is, in fact, a Lutheran Swede). When I say, "Being Italian is not the blood in your veins, but the spirit in your heart," Phil exemplifies that statement. He is also a 20-year restaurant industry veteran, who at the time Buca Little Italy was founded was already known for the wonderful restaurants he had created in Minneapolis–St. Paul. ✻ ✻ ✻ Our venture started humbly. During a family vacation to Southern Italy, the Roberts family dined at many traditional "bucas." Phil was impressed, not only by the food and wine, but by the sense of community the restaurants created: people—neighbors, families and strangers alike—sharing the dining experience. And the vision was born. ✻ ✻ ✻ The creative pieces came together for him like a puzzle. A restaurant that was comfortable, much like dining at Grandma's— from the delicious food to some of her decorating sensibilities. A restaurant with the immigrant's influence. A true "buca," much like the original mom-and-pop joints of Little Italy in New York, Philadelphia and, like my family's restaurant in Cleveland. In true Southern Italian tradition, it would have a menu where the red sauce is the lifeblood. And, of course, a place where the mouthwatering food is served family-style to encourage sharing and create a sense of community. ✻ ✻ ✻ And Buca Little Italy was born, a kitschy, eclectic restaurant in the basement of an apartment building at 12th and Harmon in Minneapolis with menus on the wall featuring classic dishes: Spaghetti Meatballs, Chicken Cacciatore, Chicken Parmigiana, Ravioli al Pomodoro, Garlic Bread and the like (all courtesy of his longtime associate, Vittorio Renda, executive chef). ✻ ✻ ✻ It's Phil's vision and my immigrant spirit that our guests experience today—from the gusto with which we serve our food to the humor in our décor. Our restaurants share exactly the type of larger-than-life yet completely comfortable atmosphere he wanted to create. ✻ ✻ ✻ When it came time to expand and grow Buca Little Italy, the doors opened for me to join Phil and become part of this wonderful organization, and together we created Buca di Beppo and, soon after, BUCA, Inc. Thank you, Phil, for allowing me to share the Buca di Beppo experience.

Joseph P. Micatrotto, BUCA, Inc., Chairman, President and CEO

Foreward

Foreward * * * I was not born Italian. But if you are what you eat, then I am Italian from head to toe, and Southern Italian at that. Red sauce flows in my veins which are, in turn, made of pasta. Large parts of me are chicken, other parts are veal; meatballs are scattered everywhere. If I cut myself you can smell the garlic; I suspect my brain is mostly Parmigiano-Reggiano, which must be why I'm so smart, for it is a wise man who eats as much Italian cheese as he can.

Buca di Beppo is like the food I grew up eating in the Bronx, only better. My mother had a rare talent as a cook; the singular ability to remove all flavor from whatever she prepared; to this day, I've never figured out how she did it. Under her tutelage, eating was an exercise in vehicle maintenance, only not as much fun. It wasn't until I went to elementary school, to P.S. 11 on Ogden Avenue in the Highbridge Section of the Bronx, that I discovered that food does not have to taste like dust. I discovered Italian cooking.

It was at a restaurant called Three Sarges. Three Sarges was opened, as were so many New York Italian eateries, by soldiers—in this case three sergeants—returning from World War II. They made pizza. They cooked spaghetti and meatballs. They baked steaming pans of lasagne. They didn't know from carpaccio— what they knew was tomato sauce and olive oil. For a quarter I could get a slice of cheese pizza and a soda from them. It was a taste of manna. It was heaven. It was sublime. It transformed me. I had found religion.

As I grew in gustatory experience, I discovered the wonders of restaurants like Mario's, Roberto's and Dominick's on Arthur Avenue, the Little Italy of the Bronx. In college I moved to the Village, a short stroll from the Little Italy of Mulberry and Hester Streets, where I spent many happy evenings eating at Puglia, a Southern Italian restaurant with long tables, wine with no labels and a concertina player who could perform everything from "That's Amore" to "Stairway to Heaven." I went west young man to San Francisco where I lived on a diet of red sauce and cappuccino. And then I relocated to Los Angeles, a city without a Little Italy, where finding a good hunk of mortadella or provolone was not an easy task.

Over the years, I haven't just feasted to joyous excess on the exuberant cooking at Buca di Beppo, I've also had the tasty pleasure of getting to know many of the people who make the restaurant what it is, like red sauce cowboys Joe Micatrotto and Vittorio Renda. In addition to revealing culinary secrets formerly guarded by a blood oath, this book gives you a chance to hear some of the family stories, legends and lore that are part of the history of Buca di Beppo. In this volume, secrets are revealed, mysteries are unlocked, puzzles are solved. At heart, this isn't a cookbook—it's a guide to being Italian, to living, loving and eating Italian. All you have to supply is an appetite for enjoyment!

Merrill Shindler
CBS Radio, Zagat Restaurant Survey

CONTENTS

When Nicolangelo Iammarino decided to leave his village near Campobasso for a better life abroad, he had a choice.

Others before him had emigrated to Canada. Some sailed south to Argentina. And still others headed to the United States, many of them settling in Cleveland, where steel mills and foundries paid decent wages for grueling work.

My grandfather chose America. And in that moment almost a century ago, before he left the boot of Italy, before he ever saw the port of Naples or the Main Hall at Ellis Island, Nick altered the course not only of his life, but of countless others: the lives of his wife and children, who helped him create Iammarino Catering in the basement of his apartment building; the lives of his grandchildren (including those of us whose careers in the restaurant industry were preordained), and eventually the lives of every member of the Buca di Beppo *famiglia*.

Now Nick has come into your life—and he's beckoning you *Into the Sauce*. In fact, that's my grandfather on the cover of this book. If you look closely, you can see my mother standing behind him. If they had wide-angle lenses back then, you'd probably see me, too—one hand on her apron, the other holding a piece of pizza half in my hand and half on my shirt. And if you pulled back a bit farther, you'd see the stove. At least three burners would be going—boiling water for pasta, sautéeing mushrooms and simmering the sauce. Always the sauce.

If Nick wasn't cooking for his family, he was cooking for his guests, for his *paisans*, and sometimes literally the entire neighborhood. After all, who could resist the aroma of a Bolognese that had been stewing since morning, a marinara whipped up in the middle of a card game or a mushroom-and-pepper-laden cacciatore?

Populated by Poles, Germans, Jews, Greeks and Italians, our corner of Cleveland was indeed a melting pot, but what brought people together in the heart of our neighborhood was my grandfather's stewpot. I used to wonder how it was that everyone loved his food—even the bacalà!—when half of them weren't even Italian like we were. How did our house become a gathering place for the whole neighborhood? And how come the conversation and laughter went on so late that sometimes it woke me from my sleep?

He just smiled, but I could read the answer in his eyes: "It's not the blood in your veins that makes you Italian, but the spirit in your heart." My grandfather had that spirit. And it spilled over from every platter he served.

"Buca di Beppo" translates into "Joe's basement," but it was my grandfather who introduced me to the warmth and flavor of the immigrant Southern Italian kitchen. He was also the one who convinced me there was no better business than his. "If you make food people like," he'd tell me, "they will pay you money and they'll pay you compliments. What else is there?" Sure enough, after spending my childhood and teenage years working in the family business, I embarked on

my trek to college and then on to my own career in the restaurant industry.

Yet I didn't exactly pick up where my grandfather left off. Though I grew up in an Italian kitchen, married a good Catholic girl (my wonderful wife, Connie) and of course reared my two sons to sop up a Bolognese as expertly as their father, it took a non-Italian to bring me back *Into the Sauce*.

In 1996, I met restaurateur and entrepreneur Phil Roberts, founder of a tiny basement restaurant in Minneapolis not so different from my grandfather's. Phil didn't have an ounce of Italian blood, but the immigrant spirit had long since claimed his soul. Buca Little Italy was his love letter to immigrant Southern Italian cooking. That was also when I met Vittorio Renda, the Calabrian-born executive chef of Buca di Beppo, my collaborator on this book, the source of many of its recipes and an effusive, passionate champion of the Southern Italian kitchen.

Just as tomatoes, garlic and olive oil are the pillars of Southern Italian cooking, we represented the three faces of Italian

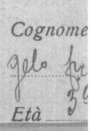

immigration. Vittorio is the freshly arrived immigrant, demonstrating the continuing influence of the Old Country. Phil was the convert, seduced by the spirit of Southern Italy. And I'm the son and grandson of immigrants, building on the legacy my grandfather created in the basement of 2192 Murray Hill Road in Cleveland's Little Italy. The spirit of Buca di Beppo is expressed in everything we do. It's in the art on our walls, which critics call campy but which actually includes many photos of old friends and family. The spirit of Buca di Beppo is in our meatballs, perhaps the perfect symbol of Italian-American immigrant cooking. The spirit of Buca di Beppo is also in our wine (displayed in the classic wicker baskets so beloved by Americans), authentic regional varietals representing the best of Italian winemaking.

Each of us lives in this cookbook—and no one more than Nicolangelo Iammarino. Yet, every immigrant can lay claim to the spirit and the passion that gave birth to this book. The spirit of Buca di Beppo is what you take away from the table at the end of the meal: a sense of joy, of bounty and, most of all, of belonging to the Buca di Beppo famiglia. The wealth of the immigrant kitchen belongs to all of us, and it enriches our country beyond measure. Buca di Beppo feeds America's hunger for community, and when you leave our red-checked tablecloths behind you're taking home your place in the Southern Italian immigrant experience. *Into the Sauce* captures the flavor of the very first "buca" I ever knew. When you create your own little "Buca di *your house*" with these recipes, we hope you remember that it's not only the food on your table that makes the meal, it's the spirit in your heart.

Like our restaurants, this cookbook was born not in a boardroom, but in front of a stove. And it's my honor and privilege to share that heritage, from our cucina to your kitchen. *Buon appetito*!

Joseph P. Micatrotto, BUCA, Inc.,
Chairman, President and CEO

Opposite page: Joe and Vittorio show off fresh ingredients—the "diamonds" of the Italian kitchen.

13

Diamonds

OF THE

ITALIAN KITCHEN

Bruschetta Salvatore

Sweet Pepper Stew

Fresh Fennel Salad

Green Beans with Lemon and
Fried Prosciutto

Fresh Fig and Prosciutto Salad

Risotto con Porcini

San Vito Mozzarella Caprese

Homemade Crusty Bread

Stuffed Zucchini Blossoms

Lentil Soup

Whenever we open a new Buca di Beppo restaurant, two things happen before we serve a single plate of spaghetti: A priest blesses the building, and Vittorio Renda, executive chef, blesses the kitchen. That means working side-by-side with the chefs he entrusts to cook for our guests. * When I teach new members of the *famiglia* about our food, says Vittorio, I try to explain what my father, Martino, taught me about ingredients: They're the stars—the diamonds—of the Italian kitchen. When you go to the market to buy your ingredients, choose only the best. Smell them, touch them. Let other people squeeze the Charmin; you squeeze the tomato. Maybe people will look at you funny, but take your time and search out *il migliore* ('the best'), because what comes out of the kitchen is only as good as what you bring in. * Pick up your tomato. It has to be ripe, not too mushy, not too hard. Did you look at the color? Now give it a gentle squeeze—that will tell you what kind of dish it's meant for. A tomato that's a little hard is good for a bruschetta. One that's a little too ripe is good for sauce. But a tomato that's perfect? That's what you want for salad. * The most important thing a cook can learn is to be mindful of your ingredients. That way, when you're cooking, you know how to change what you do a little this way, a little that way, to use the strength of your ingredients. * Here's a general rule for Italian cooking: What you're using should smell so good you want to eat it plain. The tomatoes smell sweet, the basil smells fresh—even the onion, you want to eat it like an apple! Trust your senses, and the goodness of your ingredients will come through in every dish you prepare. Your ingredients are your diamonds. Let them shine.

Baked
Specialties

$22.95
BAKED RAVIOLI

STUFFED SHELLS

BAKED MANICOTTI

BUCA BIANCO WINE
GOES GREAT WITH ANY
OF OUR BAKED SPECIALS

Vittorio's Roots

"You know the boot of Italy? I'm from the toe," says Vittorio. "Calabria is the tip of the country, one of the poorest parts of Italy—but also one of the richest.

"My father did the cooking for our family, and every meal began with a trip to the garden. As I followed him from the kitchen to the field behind our house, he would say to me: 'We may not have a lot of money in the bank, but we are truly rich. Here are our diamonds: our peppers, tomatoes, garlic.' He was right; we were dirt poor, but just look at what the dirt produced! When you put a great meal on the table, when you're happy to see each other, when you have such a good meal, you really are rich. It's your life, your time with your family, with the people you love. That's what truly matters.

"I came to the United States in 1980, to be a chef. When I came to Buca di Beppo, my roots and my family in Italy became an important part of what I do in the kitchen and what I try to explain to our famiglia and guests.

"Whether you're eating at Buca di Beppo or in your own kitchen, I want you to taste the diamonds in every dish. That's why we make everything from scratch, every day— the marinara, the meatballs, even the vinaigrette on the *insalata*. By cooking this way, everyone feels like they are being showered with diamonds, and that's the way it can be at your kitchen table, too.

"When you take the best ingredients and cook with passion, the result will always be the best food you ever tasted, a treasure for you to enjoy with your family and friends. Then you are truly rich." ✳

Vittorio's father, Martino Renda. Opposite page: Vittorio presents some of Buca di Beppo restaurants' famous cannelloni.

Bruschetta Salvatore

6 slices Italian bread, 1/2-inch thick

Salt to taste

6 slices fresh eggplant,
   1/4-inch-thick pieces sliced lengthwise

3/4 cup olive oil

3 medium-size fresh tomatoes, diced

1/2 medium-size red onion, chopped

2 tablespoons chopped fresh basil

1 tablespoon minced garlic

Pepper to taste

6 ounces soft goat cheese

4 ounces fresh mozzarella cheese,
   diced into 1/4-inch cubes

* * * * *

Preheat oven to 350 degrees and bake bread until light brown; set aside. (For faster browning, use a toaster.) Salt the eggplant slices on both sides and let stand for about 30 minutes, then pat eggplant dry. Put 1/4 cup of olive oil in a sauté pan and over medium heat fry the eggplant on both sides until it is light brown. Set aside. In a bowl, mix the tomatoes, 1/2 cup olive oil, onion, basil, garlic, salt and pepper, creating a bruschetta mix. Place the bread on a small sheet pan. Spread the goat cheese evenly on the toasted bread. Place the eggplant on top of the goat cheese. Top with the bruschetta mix. Sprinkle the fresh mozzarella cheese over the top. Put the bruschetta under the broiler for 2 to 3 minutes, until the mozzarella cheese is light golden brown. Serve immediately.

Makes 6 bruschetta.

✿✿

"Antipasto" literally means "before the pasta," but it refers to any collection of hot or cold dishes served as appetizers. For no-fuss entertaining in the Italian tradition, consider filling a sideboard or table with a variety of breads and breadsticks, spreads, salads, cheeses such as Taleggio and Parmigiano-Reggiano, thinly sliced meats such as prosciutto and salami, as well as make-ahead rustic treats like this Sweet Pepper Stew.

Sweet Pepper Stew

(Peperonata)

1/2 medium-size red onion, julienned

2 tablespoons chopped garlic

1/4 cup olive oil

4 sweet bell peppers (green, red, yellow), cleaned and julienned

2 tablespoons capers

1 (14 1/2–ounce) can plum tomatoes with juice, chopped

Salt to taste

Pepper to taste

In a large brazier over medium heat, sauté the onion and garlic in the olive oil until translucent. Add the peppers and cook until soft, approximately 10 minutes. Add the capers, tomatoes, salt and pepper. Turn the heat to low and cook until the peppers and tomatoes are a soft stew consistency, about 25 minutes. Remove from the heat, place on a serving platter and serve as a side dish. Peperonata can also be served at room temperature.

Serves 4 to 6.

✿✿✿✿✿✿✿✿✿✿✿✿✿✿✿✿✿   ✿✿✿✿✿✿✿✿✿✿✿✿✿✿✿✿

✳✳✳

Fresh Fennel Salad
(Insalata di Finocchi)

2 large bulbs fresh fennel

1 small head romaine lettuce, chopped

1/4 cup raisins

1/2 pound small red grapes, halved

2 large oranges, peeled and segmented

1/2 cup olive oil

1/4 cup balsamic vinegar or good wine vinegar

Salt to taste

Pepper to taste

1 tablespoon chopped garlic

1/2 cup ricotta salata, chopped

Discard the core and top greens from the fennel bulbs, wash the fennel and cut in half. Cut each half into thin slices and place them in a large mixing bowl. Add lettuce, raisins, grapes, oranges, olive oil, vinegar, salt, pepper and garlic. Mix well. Divide the salad onto serving dishes and top each portion with crumbled ricotta salata. Serve.

Serves 4 to 6.

✳✳✳✳✳✳✳✳✳✳✳✳✳✳✳✳✳ ✳✳✳✳✳✳✳✳✳✳✳✳✳✳✳

❀❀❀❀❀❀❀❀❀❀❀❀❀❀❀❀❀❀❀❀❀❀❀❀❀❀❀❀❀❀❀❀❀❀❀❀

Green Beans with Lemon and Fried Prosciutto

(Fagiolini con Limone e Prosciutto)

1/2 cup olive oil
4 to 6 ounces prosciutto,
   thinly sliced and julienned
6 tablespoons extra-virgin olive oil
1/4 cup fresh lemon juice
Salt to taste
1 pound fresh green beans, trimmed
Lemon wedges for garnish

* * * * *

Heat the 1/2 cup olive oil in a sauté pan until hot, then add prosciutto and fry until crisp. Drain on paper towel; set aside. Discard cooking oil.

In a large mixing bowl, combine the extra-virgin olive oil, lemon juice and salt. Mix well and set aside.

In a large pot of boiling water, cook the green beans until firm to the bite, but not overcooked. Drain the beans and add to the bowl with the olive oil and lemon mixture. Toss well. Place on a serving platter, top with the fried prosciutto and garnish with the lemon wedges. Serve immediately.

Serves 4 to 6.

❀❀❀❀❀❀❀❀❀❀❀❀❀❀   ❀❀❀❀❀❀❀❀❀❀❀❀❀

Two fig varieties dominate American markets: Mission figs, which are dark purple and taste a bit like honey; and Calimyrna figs, which are a golden yellowish green and richly fruity. Either will work for this recipe; just be sure to avoid bruised or shriveled figs. Serve at room temperature.

Fresh Fig and Prosciutto Salad
(Fichi e Prosciutto Insalata)

2 medium-size Belgian endive, sliced

12 fresh figs, cut in half

2 tablespoons chopped fresh mint

1/4 cup extra-virgin olive oil

2 tablespoons balsamic vinegar

4 to 6 ounces prosciutto, sliced paper thin

Parmigiano-Reggiano cheese,
   shaved for garnish

In a large mixing bowl, combine the endive, figs, mint, olive oil and balsamic vinegar. Toss very gently, making sure not to break the figs.

Divide the prosciutto onto 4 plates and place equal helpings of salad on top of the prosciutto. Garnish each salad with cheese and serve.

Serves 4.

Risotto con Porcini

2 ounces dried porcini mushrooms
1/2 cup diced yellow onion
1/2 cup (1 stick) butter
1 1/2 cups Arborio rice
1/2 cup white wine
1 cup grated Parmigiano-Reggiano cheese
Salt to taste
Pepper to taste

* * * * *

Soak the porcini mushrooms in 4 to 5 cups of warm water for approximately 30 minutes. Strain through cheesecloth, reserving the liquid, and set aside. Place reserved liquid on the stove over low heat to keep it warm. Chop the softened mushrooms into pieces. In a large brazier, sauté the onion in the butter until translucent. Add the rice and cook until rice is opaque, about 3 minutes. Add the white wine and stir until all of the wine has been absorbed. Slowly add 1/2 cup of mushroom liquid and continue stirring until all of the juice has been absorbed. Repeat the process until the rice is just cooked to al dente and covered in a creamy sauce, about 30 minutes. Remove the brazier from the stove, add the mushrooms and half of the cheese, stir well and season with salt and pepper. Place the risotto in a serving bowl, sprinkle with the rest of the cheese and serve.

Serves 4 to 6.

Buffalo mozzarella is the incredible fresh cheese made from the milk of water buffaloes, imported to Italy. The world's best comes from San Vito, near Naples in Southern Italy (a location Joe, Phil and Vittorio visit at least twice a year). In the United States, no matter how hard you look, you won't find a cheese exactly the same as the buffalo mozzarella from San Vito, but an equivalent version made from local cow's milk is called fiore di latte. Look for it in a specialty store.

San Vito Mozzarella Caprese

1 pound fresh buffalo mozzarella cheese
  or fresh milk mozzarella cheese, sliced
1 pound fresh Roma (or any good, ripe
  summer) tomatoes, quartered
Salt to taste
Pepper to taste
1/4 cup extra-virgin olive oil
1 tablespoon chopped fresh basil
8 fresh basil leaves

Place sliced fresh mozzarella cheese in two rows down the middle of a large serving platter. On each side of the mozzarella cheese lay quartered tomatoes. Sprinkle salt over the tomatoes and fresh mozzarella cheese. Top with lots of pepper. Evenly pour the olive oil over the tomatoes and mozzarella cheese. Top with chopped fresh basil. Garnish with basil leaves. For best results, prepare 30 minutes before serving. Serve at room temperature.

Serves 4 to 6.

This photo, which was taken on one of the Buca di Beppo famiglia journeys to Italy, shows the making of fresh buffalo mozzarella cheese in San Vito.

Homemade Crusty Bread
(Pane Casareccio)

1 1/2 cups water, warmed to 100 degrees
1/4-ounce envelope dry instant yeast
1 1/2 teaspoons salt
5 cups bread flour (plus extra for
   kneading and baking)
Olive oil, for oiling the bowl
Baking stone

* * * * *

Place the warm water and yeast in the bowl of a large electric mixer. When the yeast is dissolved add the salt and half of the flour. Mix well on low speed to blend gradually. Add the rest of the flour, using the dough hook to mix, until the sides of mixing bowl are clean and the dough is smooth and elastic. Put dough in a large mixing bowl that has been brushed with olive oil, cover with plastic wrap and place in a warm spot to rise until the dough doubles in volume, approximately 1 1/2 hours.

On a work surface sprinkled with flour, knead dough until firm. Form the dough into a ball shape and flatten. Place the dough on a sheet pan, sprinkle with flour, cover loosely with plastic wrap and place in a warm spot. Let the dough rise until it increases in volume by half, about 1 hour.

Place baking stone on the oven's bottom rack. (Baking stones mimic the dry heat of a brick oven, resulting in a rustic loaf.) Preheat oven to 400 degrees. Bake the bread directly on the stone until golden brown, about 45 minutes. Place the bread on a cooling rack for about 2 hours.

This crusty bread can be enjoyed dipped into extra-virgin olive oil, grilled and used to make bruschetta or sliced for sandwiches.

Makes one 28-ounce loaf.

✿✿✿✿✿✿✿✿✿✿✿✿✿✿✿✿✿✿✿✿✿✿✿✿✿✿✿✿✿✿✿✿✿✿✿✿✿✿

Stuffed Zucchini Blossoms
(Fiori di Zucchini Ripieni)

1/2 cup plus 1 tablespoon olive oil

1 large red onion, chopped

1 1/4 cups plain dry bread crumbs

1 (14 1/2-ounce) can plum tomatoes
   with juice, chopped

3 tablespoons capers

1/3 cup grated Pecorino Romano cheese

1 medium-size ball fresh mozzarella
   cheese, diced

2 large eggs, lightly beaten

1 garlic clove, minced

Salt to taste

Pepper to taste

16 large zucchini blossoms (without fruit)

1/4 cup white wine

8 lemon wedges

* * * * *

Preheat oven to 350 degrees. Coat an
oval baking dish, approximately 6 by

10 inches, with 1 tablespoon olive oil. In a
heavy large skillet, heat the remaining 1/2
cup olive oil. Add the onion and sauté until
translucent. Add 1 cup of bread crumbs and
stir until the bread crumbs are toasted and
golden brown. Transfer to a large bowl and
cool. Mix in the tomatoes and their juice,
capers, Romano cheese, mozzarella cheese,
eggs, garlic, salt and pepper.

Use a tablespoon to fill the zucchini
blossoms with the bread-crumb mixture,
being careful not to tear the blossoms.
Place the zucchini blossoms in the baking
dish, drizzle with white wine and top with
the remaining 1/4 cup of bread crumbs.
Bake until zucchini blossoms are tender and
bread crumbs are brown, approximately 30
minutes. Serve with lemon wedges.

Serves 6 to 8.

Opposite page: The Florence market—
a must-see stop when in Italy.

✿✿✿✿✿✿✿✿✿✿✿✿✿✿✿✿✿   ✿✿✿✿✿✿✿✿✿✿✿✿✿✿✿✿

❀❀

Lentil Soup
(Zuppa di Lenticchie)

3 quarts veal or beef stock
1 pound dried lentils, rinsed
1 large carrot, finely diced
1 yellow onion, finely diced
1/2 cup finely diced celery
1 pound Italian sausage, cooked
   and coarsely chopped
3 tablespoons chopped fresh sage
1 cup chopped ripe tomatoes
Salt to taste
Pepper to taste
Extra-virgin olive oil for garnish

Bring the stock to a boil,
then add the lentils, carrot, onion,
celery, sausage and sage. Turn
heat down to medium and cook for
approximately 1 hour or until the
soup thickens. Stir in the tomatoes,
salt and pepper. Serve the soup in
individual bowls, topping with
extra-virgin olive oil.

Serves 6 to 8.

❀❀❀❀❀❀❀❀❀❀❀❀❀❀❀❀❀❀❀❀❀   ❀❀❀❀❀❀❀❀❀❀❀❀❀❀❀

SPAGHETTI,

SAUCE

AND

Spaghetti Sauce!

Spaghetti with Garlic Oil and Vegetables

Marinara Sauce

Spaghetti and Meatballs

Tomato Meat Sauce

Alfredo Sauce

Linguine with Seafood

Seafood Linguine with Pesto Sauce

Little Hat Pasta with Spicy Chicken

Penne Calabrese

Young boys carry poles of spaghetti into a factory yard for drying. Opposite page: Joe and his parents in their Easter Day finest outside the family restaurant in Cleveland's Little Italy.

Marco Polo did not introduce Italians to pasta. He may have brought some back from China, but ancient tomb carvings prove that the Etruscans, the people who lived in Italy even before the Romans, were combining wheat, eggs and water long before Marco Polo tasted his first noodle.

That means that centuries before Christ, Italians were perfecting pasta; by the time the tomatoes Columbus brought back from America became popular in Italy in the 17th century, pasta was the main foodstuff of Southern Italy, where the combination of hot sun and drying Mediterranean breezes created an ideal environment to dry pasta.

Italians have always felt passionate about these life-sustaining noodles. It is said that macaroni derives from *"ma, che carini!"*— "My, what little dears!" Many common pasta names are equally loving: linguine is "little tongues" and ziti is "little bridegrooms."

"I think I've been around the making of pasta since I was eight," says Joe. "You mix semolina, eggs and

water, then knead it for a little bit, let it rise, take the rolling pin and roll it out, feed it through the machine—that's the whole process. Maybe you'd make spaghetti; maybe you'd take a little spoon and weigh out the filling, making raviolis. When my family came over from Campobasso in Southern Italy, they had very little money, but they were very rich in their dreams. Pasta was always an important part of our daily life. My grandfather would say, '*En vita, pasta*'—pasta is alive. The way rice is ubiquitous in Eastern Asia, pasta was the foundation, it was the earth.

"And the sauce was your genealogy. It was your province, your city, your street— your family pedigree. Sauce is the lifeblood of Italy, and it changes as you move from town to town. In rich northern cities there's plenty of meat in the sauce, while down south you might have more oregano, because of the Greek influence. Tell me what you put on your pasta, and I'll tell you who you are and where you are from." ❊

Al dente means "to the tooth" and is the phrase Italians use to describe pasta that isn't soft or overcooked, but offers a bit of resistance to the teeth when you bite into it. How do you get a perfect al dente noodle? There's no strict rule, because different sorts of pasta require different cooking times—a handful of fresh angel hair in a lot of water could be al dente in a minute; dried radiatori will take quite a bit longer. Two rules of thumb will help you master the art: First, remember that pasta will continue to cook during the time it takes you to get your potholders together, move and drain the pasta. Second, when working with an unfamiliar pasta, taste it every few moments toward the end of cooking, to learn how it changes. The truth of the matter is that you'll get a good al dente noodle only one way: Practice, practice, practice!

Spaghetti with Garlic Oil and Vegetables

(Spaghetti Aglio Olio Peperoncino)

1/3 cup olive oil

1 cup julienned red onion

1 1/2 cups carrot coins

3 cups fresh small mushrooms sliced into halves

2 cups zucchini coins

3 tablespoons chopped garlic

1 teaspoon salt

1/2 teaspoon crushed red pepper flakes

1 pound spaghetti

1 cup grated Pecorino Romano cheese

In a large pan over medium heat, sauté in olive oil the onion, carrots, mushrooms, zucchini and garlic until light brown, then add the salt and crushed red pepper flakes. Keep warm.

Cook the spaghetti in plenty of boiling water until al dente. Add 1 cup of spaghetti water to the vegetables. Drain the spaghetti, add the vegetable sauce and half of the cheese; toss well. Divide into 4 to 6 serving bowls, making sure to evenly divide the vegetables. Sprinkle the remaining cheese over the top. Serve hot.

Serves 4 to 6.

Many Italians believe a marinara sauce should be as individual as a fingerprint, so they add little flourishes, like adding a grated carrot, substituting butter for oil or finishing with a spoonful of parsley pesto. What will your fingerprint be?

Marinara Sauce

1/4 cup olive oil

1 red onion, chopped

6 garlic cloves, chopped

2 (28-ounce) cans
    crushed tomatoes

Salt to taste

3 tablespoons chopped
    fresh basil

In a 3-quart saucepan, heat the olive oil over medium heat. Add the onion and garlic, and cook until golden brown, approximately 8 to 10 minutes. Add the tomatoes and salt. Bring to a boil, then cook over low heat for approximately 30 minutes, stirring often. Turn off the heat and add the fresh basil.

Yields about 6 cups.

※ ※

At Buca di Beppo we slow simmer our meatballs in our Marinara Sauce. Everything you put in your meatball comes through, because you don't dry them out by baking them.

Spaghetti and Meatballs
(Spaghetti con Polpette)

2 1/2 pounds ground beef
1/2 cup grated Pecorino Romano cheese
3/4 cup dry Italian-style bread crumbs
4 large eggs
1/4 cup chopped garlic
2 teaspoons salt
Meatball Sauce (see recipe on page 48)
1 pound spaghetti
1/4 cup grated Parmigiano-Reggiano cheese
1/4 cup chopped fresh basil

* * * * *

In a large mixing bowl, combine ground beef, Romano cheese, bread crumbs, eggs, garlic and salt; mix well. Shape into meatballs the size of golf balls. Use all of the meat mixture (makes about 40 meatballs). Set meatballs aside and let rest for approximately 1 hour.

Cook the meatballs in the Meatball Sauce.

In a large pot of boiling water, cook the spaghetti until al dente, then drain. Toss the pasta with some of the sauce. To serve, place spaghetti in individual bowls and then spoon meatballs and more sauce on top. Garnish with Parmesan cheese and fresh basil.

Note: Leftover sauce can be saved in refrigerator for later use.

Serves 6.

※ ※ ※ ※ ※ ※ ※ ※ ※ ※ ※ ※ ※ ※ ※ ※ ※   ※ ※ ※ ※ ※ ※ ※ ※ ※ ※ ※ ※ ※ ※ ※ ※

Meatball Sauce

6 garlic cloves, sliced thinly
1 large Spanish onion,
   diced into 1/4-inch pieces
1 celery stalk, chopped
1 carrot, chopped
1/4 cup plus 2 tablespoons
   olive oil
1/4 cup chopped fresh
   Italian parsley
2 (28-ounce) cans plum tomatoes
   with juice
Salt to taste
Pepper to taste
Meatballs (see recipe on page 46)

In a large pan or heatproof casserole, sauté over medium heat the garlic, onion, celery and carrot in the olive oil until translucent. Add the parsley. Break up the tomatoes with your hands and add, with all of the tomato juice, to the pan. Add salt and pepper. Bring to a boil, then lower the heat and add the meatballs. Be prepared: sauce will significantly increase in volume, but then it will reduce back by one-third by the end of the cooking time, approximately 45 minutes. Remove meatballs from sauce and keep warm.

Yields 6 cups.

Tomato Meat Sauce
(Sugo di Carne)

1/4 cup olive oil
1/2 cup chopped red onion
1/2 cup chopped celery
1/2 cup chopped carrot
1/4 cup chopped garlic
2 pounds ground beef
1/4 cup red wine
1 (28-ounce) can whole peeled
  tomatoes
Salt to taste
Pepper to taste

In a large pan, sauté in olive oil the onion, celery, carrot and garlic over medium heat until the onion is translucent. In another pan, brown the meat. Once meat is browned, drain off the grease and add meat to the vegetable mixture. Add the wine, reduce it by half, then add the tomatoes, salt and pepper. Cook over medium heat for approximately 30 minutes, stirring often.

This sauce can be served hot with all kinds of pasta, such as ravioli or tortellini, or it can be refrigerated and used in all kinds of baked dishes.

Yields 6 cups.

Alfredo Sauce

1 quart whipping cream
1/2 teaspoon salt
1 tablespoon butter, cubed
1/4 teaspoon white pepper
Pinch of nutmeg
2 cups grated
    Parmigiano-Reggiano cheese
3 egg yolks, beaten

* * * * *

In a large saucepan over medium heat, heat
the cream, salt, butter, white pepper and
nutmeg to 140 degrees, stirring occasionally.
Add the cheese a little at a time, stirring
constantly until cheese is completely
incorporated. Simmer for 10 minutes while
stirring. It should become thick and smooth.
Temper egg yolks (to prevent curdling) by
placing them in a cup or bowl and gradually
adding a little of the hot sauce. Stir this
into the rest of sauce, and cook for a few
more minutes. Do not boil. Use immediately
or cool in the refrigerator.

This cream sauce is an alternative
to red sauce for pastas. For best results,
use the alfredo sauce with fresh pastas
such as fettuccine, pappardelle, ravioli
and tortellini. It can also be transformed
into a walnut or pistachio sauce by adding
plenty of toasted, chopped nuts.

Yields 5 cups.

50

Linguine with Seafood
(Linguine allo Scoglio)

1/4 cup olive oil

2 tablespoons chopped garlic

1/2 pound mussels, scrubbed
and debearded

1/2 pound Manila clams, scrubbed

1/2 pound squid, sliced into rings,
tentacles cut in half

1/2 pound medium shrimp,
peeled and deveined

1/2 cup white wine

Salt to taste

2 teaspoons crushed red pepper flakes

1 (28-ounce) can Italian plum
tomatoes with juice, crushed

1 pound linguine

2 tablespoons chopped
fresh Italian parsley

Heat the olive oil in a large saucepan over medium-high heat; add the garlic and brown. Add the mussels, clams, squid, shrimp and wine. Cook until the mussels and clams open, releasing their juices, about 4 minutes. Add the salt and crushed red pepper flakes. Cook until the wine is reduced by half; add the tomatoes. Bring to a boil, then reduce heat and cook for approximately 10 minutes.

Meanwhile, bring a pot of water to a boil and cook the linguine until al dente. Drain pasta and place it on a large serving plate. Top with the seafood sauce and finish with the chopped parsley.

Serves 4 to 6.

✄ ✄

Seafood Linguine with Pesto Sauce

(Linguine con Pesto Sorrento)

1 cup dry white wine

1/2 pound whole bay scallops

1/2 pound medium shrimp,
   peeled and deveined

3/4 pound squid, sliced into rings,
   tentacles cut in half

1 cup Pesto Sauce
   (see recipe on page 55)

1 pound linguine

1 cup heavy cream

1/2 cup grated Pecorino Romano cheese

Salt to taste

In a large sauté pan over medium heat, heat the white wine. Add the scallops, shrimp and squid. Poach for approximately 5 minutes, add Pesto Sauce, mix well and keep warm.

In the meantime, in a pot of boiling water, cook the linguine until al dente, then drain and add to the seafood. Toss with cream, cheese and salt. Serve immediately.

Serves 4.

✄ ✄ ✄ ✄ ✄ ✄ ✄ ✄ ✄ ✄ ✄ ✄ ✄ ✄ ✄ ✄      ✄ ✄ ✄ ✄ ✄ ✄ ✄ ✄ ✄ ✄ ✄ ✄ ✄ ✄ ✄

Pesto comes from the Italian word *pestare*, which means "to pound or bruise." Traditionally, you'd place your ingredients in a mortar and pestle (also from *pestare*) and pound them into a paste (guess where that word comes from?).

Pesto Sauce

4 ounces fresh basil leaves

2 tablespoons chopped garlic

1 ounce pine nuts

1 cup olive oil

2 tablespoons butter

1 cup grated Pecorino Romano cheese

1 cup grated Parmigiano-Reggiano cheese

1 teaspoon pepper

Salt to taste

Run the basil, garlic, pine nuts, olive oil and butter through a food mill or pound with a mortar and pestle. Alternatively, use the chopping blade of a food processor. Place in a large bowl. Add the remaining ingredients, mix well and refrigerate in a tightly sealed container. Take the amount of pesto needed and bring to room temperature approximately 30 minutes before use.

Yields 2 cups.

Orecchiette pasta is a staple in the Puglia region,
which is in the hills in the boot of Italy.

Little Hat Pasta with Spicy Chicken
(Orecchiette Pugliesi)

3/4 cup olive oil

2 tablespoons chopped garlic

2 teaspoons crushed
    red pepper flakes

2 (6-ounce) boneless, skinless
    chicken breasts, diced into
    1-by-1-inch pieces

2 cups broccoli florets, blanched

1 small zucchini, thinly sliced
    and blanched

1 teaspoon salt

1 pound orecchiette

1 medium tomato, chopped

1/4 cup grated Pecorino Romano cheese

In a large sauté pan, heat the olive oil over medium heat. Add the garlic and the crushed red pepper flakes, cooking until aromatic, about 30 seconds. Add the chicken and sauté until brown. Add broccoli, zucchini and salt; cook until tender and brown, about 5 minutes. Set aside.

In a large pot of boiling water, cook the orecchiette until al dente. Prior to draining the pasta, take 1/4 cup of the hot water and add to the sauce along with the tomato. Drain the pasta very well. Place the pasta back into the pot and add the sauce and cheese. Toss very well, until the sauce is completely incorporated. Serve immediately.

Serves 4.

"The region of Calabria, where I was born, is known for its homemade sausages, ricotta salata, olive oil and Pecorino Romano cheese. The locals are lucky to have all of the homemade items available to use in their favorite dishes." —Vittorio

Penne Calabrese

1/4 cup olive oil

1/2 pound Italian bulk sausage

3 large garlic cloves, sliced

2 medium bunches escarole, chopped

2 large fresh tomatoes, diced

1/4 teaspoon crushed red
   pepper flakes

1/4 teaspoon salt

1 cup chicken stock

1 pound penne

1/4 cup grated Pecorino
   Romano cheese

1 cup ricotta salata, diced
   in 1/4-inch cubes

In a very large, deep skillet, heat olive oil and add the sausage. Brown well, breaking up the meat as it cooks. Add the garlic and cook until golden brown. Add the escarole, tomatoes, crushed red pepper flakes and salt. Sauté for a few minutes. Add chicken stock. Cook for about 15 minutes.

Meanwhile, cook the pasta in a large pot of boiling water until al dente. Drain well and add to the skillet. Sprinkle with the cheese and toss well. Place on a serving platter and garnish with ricotta salata. Serve immediately.

Serves 4.

59

Joe's family hails from
Campobasso, Italy. This
circa 1900s photo
is a town portrait.

OLD ITALIA!
New Italia!

✖ ✖ ✖ ✖ ✖ ✖ ✖ ✖

Caesar Salad with Shrimp

Beef Pizzaiola over
Garlic Mashed Potatoes

Four Cheese Risotto

Angry Stuffed Pizza

Four Seasons Pizza

Pizza Margherita

Shepherd's Pizza Roll

Veal Shank with Polenta

Beans and Pasta Soup

Chicken Saltimbocca with Escarole

Tripe for the Poor

Rigatoni with Stewed Oxtail

Between 1880 and 1930, much of Southern Italy relocated to the New World.

Whole towns packed up and left as one, transplanting entire communities to the United States, Canada and South America. In some regions, like Sicily, fully three out of five people emigrated. Along with the shirts on their backs, they brought a strong work ethic, steadfast community ties and deeply held culinary traditions.

No sooner had the immigrants resettled, however, than those traditions began to evolve. Spaghetti and pizza quickly became as American as apple pie—and eaten even more frequently by many people. Staples of the *cucina povera* (the "food for the poor"), such as pasta baked with a simple tomato sauce virtually plucked from the garden, began to incorporate expensive ingredients, including rich cheeses and meat by the mouthful. Favorite American foods also worked their way onto classic Italian-American menus.

Today, as a hundred years ago, the intertwining of Old Italia and New Italia continues. Indeed, the recipes in this book—based on old family recipes and new discoveries alike—reflect the ongoing exchange of culinary influences that make the Italian-American experience more vital and vibrant than ever. ✖

Joe (in his father's arms) poses with his family. Opposite page: Beef Pizzaiola and Garlic Mashed Potatoes.

Joe's Roots

Both sets of my grandparents came from Campobasso in Southern Italy (which, coincidentally, is a premier region for Italian pastas, and where much of our pasta comes from). My maternal grandfather, Nicolangelo Iammarino, got here first, at the age of 17. Sailing out of Naples with his *paisans*—his pals—he settled in Cleveland, Ohio. At first he painted trolley cars, but at night he cooked for his friends, and before long he was feeding half the neighborhood. A couple of decades later there I was, eight years old, helping out in the family's catering kitchen on weekends, hand-cranking lasagna and ravioli dough. There's always something important about feeding people. You remember the homemade pasta, the homemade marinara—you even remember the stain of sauce.

I'd follow my grandfather from table to table in my chef apron, rolled up at the waist because I was still a kid. He passed on more than 30 years ago, but I can still repeat verbatim things he said to me. I remember one time when I was 12 years old, I put too much water in a recipe. That mistake didn't cost us a lot of money, but it created a major pain in the neck for everybody. And he said to me in his own kindly way, "You're just trying to do your best and that's very important—actually going after what you want to do is more important than what you achieve in a single day. Trying hard, that is what is important. A great effort will eventually yield a great result—though not

"Nick" at work in his catering kitchen in Cleveland, Ohio. Opposite page: Joe today.

65

necessarily at the very moment you want it." So we made another batch.

You learn a lot in a restaurant. When I was a kid, the proudest moment for me was to have my kitchen whites on and tag along with my grandfather while he visited his tables. I'm so grateful to have had his wisdom and his love. Working with him taught me not only how to work in the kitchen, but, also, in true immigrant fashion, the value of hard work. Each day I worked with my grandfather, he put a $25 savings bond in the bank for me. Those deposits eventually became the down payment for my family's first home.

Most Buca di Beppo restaurants have photos on the walls of my family and my grandfather's friends from the old neighborhood. In

fact, I've gotten mail from people all over the country who've walked into their local Buca di Beppo restaurant and recognized my family, or theirs. "That's Joe Mic," they say, "and that's Aunt Angela and Aunt Rita right behind him!"

At Buca di Beppo we can be a little over the top, a little crazy with the fun, but I think people can tell that pretty close to the surface is a real Italian family, with real heart.

Today, every restaurant has a copy of some of my family's Ellis Island immigration papers; they might not be the first thing you see, but trust me, they're there— as a reminder of our immigrant heritage. ❊

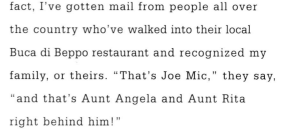

Opposite page: Joe's grandfather's immigration papers hang in every Buca di Beppo restaurant.

©BETTMANN/CORBIS

R. ISPETTORATO DELL'EMIGRAZIONE
— DI NAPOLI —
dipendente dal Commissariato Generale dell'Emigrazione

"CASA DEGLI EMIGRANTI„

Cognome, Nome, Paternità *Sammarino Nicola,*
gelo fu Giustino e famiglia
Elisa - Iris, Maria

Età *39*

In partenza il

da Napoli

per New-York

in **seconda classe**

Col Piroscafo "*DUILIO*„

29 GEN 1925

IL DIRETTORE
della R. Casa Emigranti

(data)

L'Incaricato Ro. Suora Enrichetta

Ro. Suora Enrichetta

DISINFETTAZIONE

Caesar Salad with Shrimp

(Insalata di Cesare con Gamberetti)

1/2 pound raw small shrimp,
   peeled and deveined
1/2 head romaine lettuce, chopped
1/2 head iceberg lettuce, chopped
1/2 head radicchio, chopped
1/2 cup Caesar Dressing
1 ounce Parmigiano-Reggiano cheese,
   grated
1 1/2 teaspoons pepper
4 lemon wedges
Croutons for garnish (optional)

* * * * *

Poach the shrimp in boiling water, drain and cool in the refrigerator. Wash the lettuce heads, drain, pat dry and chop. In a large bowl, mix together the lettuces, Caesar Dressing and shrimp. Divide onto four serving plates. Sprinkle with cheese and garnish with pepper, lemon wedges and croutons.

Serves 4.

Caesar Dressing

2 egg yolks
2 or 3 anchovies, rinsed and chopped
1 1/2 teaspoons Dijon mustard
1 1/2 tablespoons minced garlic
1 1/2 cups olive oil
2 tablespoons red wine vinegar
2 tablespoons fresh lemon juice
1/3 cup grated Parmigiano-Reggiano cheese
Salt to taste
Pepper to taste

* * * * *

Place the egg yolks, anchovies, mustard and garlic in a food processor or blender and, on medium speed, process the ingredients until blended. Slowly drizzle in olive oil. As the mixture begins to thicken, pour the olive oil in faster. When the dressing gets very thick, thin it with vinegar and lemon juice. Add the cheese, salt and pepper. Chill until ready to use. Dressing will keep 3 to 4 days refrigerated.

Makes 1 quart.

Beef Pizzaiola over Garlic Mashed Potatoes

(Filetto Pizzaiola con Pure di Patate)

1/2 cup olive oil
1 1/2 cups julienned red onion
1 tablespoon chopped garlic
1 tablespoon capers
1 1/2 pounds beef tenderloin tips
3/4 cup white wine
1 (28-ounce) can whole plum tomatoes
1 tablespoon dried oregano
Salt to taste
Pepper to taste
Garlic Mashed Potatoes
(see recipe on page 71)

In a large sauté pan over medium-high heat, heat the olive oil, red onion, garlic and capers. Sauté until the onions are translucent. Add the beef and cook until brown. Add the white wine and cook until the wine is reduced by half. Break up the whole tomatoes and add them to the pan along with the oregano, salt and pepper. Cook for about 20 minutes. Reduce heat to low and keep warm. Meanwhile, make the Garlic Mashed Potatoes.

Cover the bottom of a large serving platter with the mashed potatoes. Spoon the beef and sauce over the potatoes. (This sauce is also good over pasta.) Serve hot.

Serves 4.

✻ ✻

Garlic Mashed Potatoes
(Pure di Patate)

2 pounds small red-skinned
  potatoes, with skins on
1/4 cup finely chopped garlic
1 teaspoon dried oregano
1 teaspoon salt
1 cup grated Pecorino Romano cheese
1/2 cup butter, semisoft and
  cut into pieces

✻ ✻ ✻ ✻ ✻

Wash the potatoes and place them in
a large pot. Cover with cold water
and bring to a boil. Reduce heat
to low and cook until the potatoes
are tender. Drain the potatoes
and transfer to a large bowl. Add
the rest of the ingredients and
mix with a mixer, using a metal
whip attachment, until all of the
ingredients are incorporated.

Garlic Mashed Potatoes can be
served as a side dish or with any
other appropriate dish, such as
Beef Pizzaiola (see recipe on
page 70).

Serves 4.

✻ ✻

Four Cheese Risotto

(Risotto Quattro Formaggi)

1/2 cup chopped yellow onion

1/2 cup (1 stick) butter

1 1/2 cups Arborio rice

1/2 cup white wine

Few threads saffron

4 to 5 cups chicken stock, hot

2 ounces grated Pecorino
    Romano cheese

3 ounces fontina cheese,
    diced into 1/4-inch pieces

2 ounces Gorgonzola
    cheese, crumbled

3 ounces provolone cheese,
    diced into 1/4-inch pieces

Salt to taste

Pepper to taste

2 tablespoons chopped
    fresh Italian parsley

In a large saucepan over low heat, sauté the onion in the butter until translucent. Add the rice and gently cook until it is opaque and pearl-like, about 3 minutes. Add the white wine and saffron threads, and stir until wine has evaporated. Add 1/2 cup of hot chicken stock, stirring constantly with a wooden spoon and waiting until all of the stock has been absorbed before adding another 1/2 cup of stock. Repeat the process until the rice is cooked just to al dente and covered in a creamy sauce, about 30 minutes.

Turn off the heat and toss in the cheeses, salt and pepper. Mix well and divide into large bowls. Garnish with the Italian parsley. Serve immediately.

Serves 4 to 6.

Angry Stuffed Pizza

(Calzone Arrabbiato)

Baking stone
Cornmeal for dusting
1 ball Homemade Pizza Dough (see recipe
   on page 75), rolled into a 12-inch round
3 ounces mozzarella cheese, shredded
2 ounces pepperoni, sliced
4 ounces Italian bulk sausage,
   cooked and chopped
3 ounces canned artichoke
   hearts, quartered
2 1/2 cups chopped fresh tomatoes
1 teaspoon crushed red
   pepper flakes
1 tablespoon olive oil
1 to 2 tablespoons grated Pecorino
   Romano cheese
1 cup Marinara Sauce, heated
   (see recipe on page 44)

Put a pizza stone in the oven. Heat oven to 450 degrees. Liberally sprinkle cornmeal on a cutting board, pizza peel (flat wooden paddle) or the back of a cookie sheet. Place flattened pizza dough on it.

On one half of the dough place the mozzarella cheese, pepperoni, sausage, artichokes and tomatoes. Sprinkle crushed red pepper flakes evenly over all ingredients. Fold the other half of the dough over the ingredients to form a half-moon, and push down the sides of the dough to secure around the edges. Brush olive oil over the top of the calzone and sprinkle with Romano cheese.

Slide the calzone directly on the baking stone in the oven, and bake until golden brown, approximately 15 minutes. Serve immediately with a side of hot Marinara Sauce.

Makes one 12-inch calzone.

Four Seasons Pizza

(Pizza Quattro Stagioni)

Baking stone
1 ball Homemade Pizza Dough (see recipe on page 75), rolled into a 13-inch round
Cornmeal for dusting
1/2 pound mozzarella cheese, grated
1/4 pound fresh mushrooms, quartered
1/4 pound fresh Roma tomatoes, sliced
1/4 pound thinly sliced ham, cut into strips
1/2 cup marinated artichokes, quartered
1 egg yolk, unbroken
Salt to taste
Pepper to taste

Put a pizza stone in the oven.
Heat oven to 450 degrees.
Liberally sprinkle cornmeal on a cutting board, pizza peel (flat wooden paddle) or the back of a cookie sheet. Place flattened pizza dough on it. Sprinkle cheese evenly over the pizza dough, leaving a 1/2-inch border. Keeping the mushrooms, tomatoes, ham and artichokes separate, cover one-quarter of the pizza with each ingredient to represent the four seasons. Place the raw egg yolk in the center of the pizza. Season pizza with salt and pepper. Slide the pizza onto the heated pizza stone, and cook for approximately 10 minutes, or until the crust is golden brown. Serve immediately.

Makes one 13-inch pizza.

❋ ❋

Homemade Pizza Dough

2 1/2 cups water (warmed to 120 degrees)
1/4-ounce package active dry yeast
  or 1 ounce compressed yeast
2 teaspoons salt
1/4 cup olive oil, for oiling the bowl
5 to 6 cups bread flour

* * * * *

In a large bowl, stir together the water and yeast, then add the salt, olive oil and 4 cups of flour. Using your hands, work together all of the ingredients until the dough just holds its shape, adding more flour as needed. Turn the dough out onto a well-floured work surface and knead until smooth and elastic, approximately 10 minutes. Place dough into an oiled bowl, cover and let rise until doubled, about 30 minutes. Divide the dough into four equal balls and place in four slightly oiled plastic containers. Cover and refrigerate for about 3 hours. (If you want to use the dough sooner, set it out at room temperature and it will rise in about 1 hour.)

If chilled, take the dough out of the refrigerator about 45 minutes before baking the pizza, and let it warm to room temperature.

To shape dough, take one ball of dough and set it on a floured work surface. Using your fingers and working in a circular motion, flatten the ball of dough until it is 8 inches in diameter. Level the dough by giving it several pats with the palm of your hand until the dough reaches 13 inches in diameter. Supporting the dough with your palm, flip it onto a floured cookie sheet and proceed with your favorite recipe.

Makes enough dough for 4 pizzas.

❋ ❋ ❋ ❋ ❋ ❋ ❋ ❋ ❋   ❋ ❋ ❋ ❋ ❋ ❋ ❋ ❋ ❋

※ ※

Pizza Margherita, named after Queen Margherita, is the most popular Neapolitan pizza. Every Italian pizzeria has its version of the classic dish.

Pizza Margherita

Baking stone
1/2 cup canned crushed tomatoes
1 tablespoon chopped garlic
1/2 tablespoon dried oregano
1 tablespoon olive oil
Salt to taste
Cornmeal for dusting
1 ball Homemade Pizza Dough
    (see recipe on page 75), rolled into a
    13-inch oval
6 ounces fresh mozzarella cheese, sliced
2 tablespoons chopped fresh basil

* * * * *

Put a pizza stone in the oven. Heat oven to 450 degrees. In a mixing bowl, combine tomatoes, garlic, oregano, olive oil and salt. Mix well and set aside. Liberally sprinkle cornmeal on a cutting board, pizza peel (flat wooden paddle) or the back of a cookie sheet. Place flattened pizza dough on it.

Cover the pizza dough with the tomato mixture, spreading it evenly but leaving a 3/4-inch border around the edge of the pizza. Place the cheese slices on top of the tomato sauce. Slide the pizza onto the heated pizza stone in the oven. Cook the pizza for approximately 10 minutes, or until the crust is golden brown.

Garnish with the fresh basil and serve immediately.

Makes one 13-inch pizza.

※ ※ ※ ※ ※ ※ ※ ※ ※ ※ ※   ※ ※ ※ ※ ※ ※ ※ ※ ※ ※ ※

✵ ✵

"In my hometown, after World War II, shepherds would bring their homemade ricotta cheese to my father for him to use in different dishes. My father would make this stromboli for the shepherds. They would bring it with them and eat it during their long day of working in the mountains." —Vittorio

Shepherd's Pizza Roll

(Stromboli Pecoraio)

Baking stone
Cornmeal for dusting
1 ball Homemade Pizza Dough
   (see recipe on page 75), rolled into a
   13-inch rectangle
3 ounces pepperoni, thinly sliced
3 ounces mortadella cheese, thinly sliced
1/2 cup ricotta cheese
3/4 cup shredded mozzarella cheese
1/2 cup marinated red peppers, sliced
6 to 8 sun-dried tomatoes in oil, chopped
Olive oil for brushing
1 cup Marinara Sauce (see recipe on page 44)

* * * * *

Put a pizza stone in the oven and

preheat oven to 400 degrees. Liberally sprinkle cornmeal on a cutting board, pizza peel (flat wooden paddle) or the back of a cookie sheet. Flatten dough into a large oval shape. Brush dough with olive oil. Layer the meats, cheeses, peppers and tomatoes down the center of the dough (leave about 1 inch on each end for folding). Fold the lower third of the dough over the ingredients, then fold the top third to meet the bottom third and pinch together the center seam and ends, making a salami-shaped roll. Brush with olive oil and slide onto the heated pizza stone. Cook 20 minutes, or until crust is golden brown and the inside ingredients reach 160 degrees. Cut roll into 2-inch pieces and serve immediately with hot Marinara Sauce. This stromboli can also be cooled, wrapped in aluminum foil and eaten later at room temperature.

Makes one 13-inch roll.

✵ ✵ ✵ ✵ ✵ ✵ ✵ ✵ ✵   ✵ ✵ ✵ ✵ ✵ ✵ ✵ ✵ ✵

Se non sopporta
il calore
vattene dalla cucina!

In seeming agreement with
Harry Truman's demand
overhead (in Italian)—"If
you can't stand the heat, get
out of the kitchen!"—
these nuns raise a joyous
glass at the Kitchen Table.

※ ※

Veal Shank with Polenta

(Osso Buco con Polenta)

4 veal shanks, 2 inches thick

Salt for seasoning

Flour for dusting

1/2 cup olive oil

1 cup diced red onion

1 cup diced carrots

1 cup diced celery

1 (14 1/2-ounce) can whole tomatoes,
   chopped, with juice

1 tablespoon chopped fresh rosemary

Salt to taste

Pepper to taste

1 batch Instant Polenta

* * * * *

Preheat the oven to 325 degrees. Season the shanks with salt and then dust with flour. In a lidded sauté pan or heatproof casserole, sauté shanks in preheated olive oil on both sides until golden brown. Remove shanks, and pour off excess oil. In the same pan sauté the onion, carrots and celery. Add the tomatoes with juice and rosemary. Return the veal shanks to the pan and add water until it's 1/4 inch below the top of the shanks. Cover and bake in the oven for 2 hours, or until veal is tender. Remove the shanks from the sauce and keep warm. Reduce the sauce slightly if needed, then salt and pepper. Set aside. Spoon the polenta onto a large serving dish and top with shanks. Moisten with some of the sauce and serve with extra sauce alongside.

Serves 4.

Instant Polenta

6 cups chicken stock

2 cups instant polenta

4 ounces bacon, cooked crisp and chopped

1 tablespoon chopped garlic

Salt to taste

Pepper to taste

1 tablespoon chopped fresh sage

* * * * *

In a medium saucepan, bring the chicken stock to a boil, then add the polenta while slowly mixing with a wire whisk. Add the bacon, garlic, salt, pepper and sage. Cook for 5 to 7 minutes, or until thick.

※ ※ ※ ※ ※ ※ ※ ※ ※ ※ ※   ※ ※ ※ ※ ※ ※ ※ ※ ※ ※

Beans and Pasta Soup
(Pasta e Fagioli)

8 ounces dried cannellini beans

4 ounces bacon

1/4 cup olive oil

2 tablespoons chopped onion

2 tablespoons chopped celery

2 tablespoons chopped carrot

1/2 cup chopped fresh tomatoes

Salt to taste

Pepper to taste

1 cup tubetti

1/4 cup grated Pecorino Romano cheese

2 tablespoons chopped Italian parsley

* * * * *

Soak beans in water overnight. Drain, and place in a large soup pot; cover with about 3 quarts of water, and bring to a boil. Reduce heat to low and cook for approximately 2 hours. Meanwhile, fry bacon until crisp, drain excess fat and set aside. In the olive oil, sauté the onion, celery and carrot until translucent, and set aside.

When beans are soft, remove one-third of them. Puree in a blender and then return them to the pot to thicken the soup. Add the vegetables, tomatoes, bacon, salt and pepper. Mix well and keep cooking over low heat. Meanwhile, cook the tubetti until al dente. Drain the pasta, add it to soup and mix well. Pour soup into a large bowl or terrine. Sprinkle with cheese and parsley, and serve.

Serves 8.

Leftover soup can easily be refrigerated and then reheated over low for another meal.

✺ ✺

Did you know the popular dish of chicken saltimbocca means, literally, that the chicken is "jumping in the mouth"? That's because a dish this delicious gets eaten so quickly that it's almost as if the chicken is jumping into your mouth.

Chicken Saltimbocca with Escarole

(Saltimbocca di Pollo con Verdura)

1 pound escarole greens, chopped
4 (6-ounce) boneless, skinless chicken breasts
Salt to taste
Pepper to taste
2 tablespoons finely chopped fresh sage
4 slices prosciutto, thinly sliced
2 tablespoons olive oil
Flour for dusting
1/4 cup chicken stock
1/4 cup white wine
2 tablespoons fresh lemon juice
4 tablespoons unsalted butter
8 lemon wedges

* * * * *

In a pot of boiling water, cook the escarole for approximately 3 minutes, then drain, cool and squeeze out excess water. Set aside. Flatten chicken breasts to 1/8-inch thickness by pounding lightly between two sheets of wax paper. Sprinkle each piece with salt and pepper and spread each evenly with sage. Top each breast with a slice of prosciutto secured with wooden toothpicks.

Heat the olive oil in a large skillet over medium-high heat. Dust each breast with flour and place in sauté pan, prosciutto side down. Cook until golden brown. Turn chicken over, finish cooking, about 8 minutes. Place the chicken on a baking sheet and cover with foil to keep warm. Discard olive oil from sauté pan and add chicken stock, wine, lemon juice, prepared escarole, salt and pepper.

Cook for about 5 minutes, remove from heat, add the butter and mix in to thicken sauce. Place chicken on a large platter, prosciutto side up, remove toothpicks and pour sauce over. Garnish each chicken piece with 2 lemon wedges. Serve immediately.

Serves 4.

✺ ✺ ✺ ✺ ✺ ✺ ✺ ✺ ✺ ✺   ✺ ✺ ✺ ✺ ✺ ✺ ✺ ✺ ✺ ✺

Cucina povera. "Some of the traditional dishes in Southern Italy are not popular in the United States today, but were very popular with past generations. Many of these, like Trippa Povera, are classified as *cucina povera*, or "food for the poor." —Vittorio

Tripe for the Poor

(Trippa Povera)

1/2 cup dry chickpeas
1/2 cup dry black beans
1/2 cup dry cannellini beans
2 pounds tripe
1/2 cup chopped red onion
1/2 cup chopped celery
1/4 cup chopped garlic
1/2 cup olive oil
1 (28-ounce) can crushed tomatoes
1 tablespoon crushed red pepper flakes
Salt to taste

* * * * *

Soak chickpeas, black beans and cannellini beans in water overnight.

Drain the beans and place in a pot. Cover with water and bring to a boil. Reduce heat. Cook the beans until tender. Drain and set aside.

Place the tripe in a large saucepan. Cover with water. Over medium heat, boil until tender (approximately 1 hour). Cool, julienne and set aside.

In a large braising pan over medium-high heat, sauté the onion, celery and garlic in the olive oil. Add the tripe. Add 3 cups of water, tomatoes, red pepper flakes and salt. Cook covered for 1 hour over medium heat.

Reduce heat to low and add beans. Cook for approximately 30 minutes, adding more water if needed. Serve.

Serves 4.

Always a ladies' man, here Vittorio poses with a group of nuns. This photo was taken on a recent Buca di Beppo group trip to Italy.

✶ ✶

Rigatoni with Stewed Oxtail

(Coda di Bue Vaccinara con Rigatoni)

5 tablespoons olive oil
1/2 cup chopped red onion
1/2 cup chopped carrots
1/2 cup chopped celery
2 pounds oxtail, cut into 2-inch pieces
1 cup Chianti or other red wine
1 (28-ounce) can and half of a
   (14 1/2-ounce) can of whole
   plum tomatoes, with juice
Salt to taste
Pepper to taste
1 pound rigatoni pasta
1/2 cup grated Pecorino Romano cheese
1/2 cup loosely packed chopped
   fresh basil

Put the olive oil, onion, carrots and celery in a large brazier and sauté over medium-high heat until the vegetables are just tender. Add the meat and cook until browned. Add the wine and cook, scraping the brown bits from the pan with a wooden spoon, until the wine has been reduced by half. Add the tomatoes with juice, and season with salt and pepper. Reduce heat to medium-low, cover and simmer, stirring occasionally to break up the tomatoes, for about 2 hours, or until the meat is very tender. Remove the meat from the pan and keep warm. In a large pot of water, boil the rigatoni until al dente. Drain and add the tomato sauce. Toss well and place in a serving bowl; garnish with cheese and basil. Top each serving with one or two pieces of the meat. Meat is served on the bone.

Serves 4.

✶ ✶ ✶ ✶ ✶ ✶ ✶ ✶ ✶   ✶ ✶ ✶ ✶ ✶ ✶ ✶ ✶ ✶

Family

BEGINS WITH TWO

Sweetheart Tortellini

Angel Hair Pasta with Shrimp

Omelet with Escarole and Cheese

Baked Pasta

Melted Mozzarella Sandwich

Potato Tart Apulian Style

Orecchiette Pasta Salad with Vegetables

Wedding Soup

A couple meets. They date. They fall in love. They marry. The two separate individuals become a family. Sure, there is the extended network of relatives, in-laws and, later, children, but it begins with those two people. "When you're young, you're figuring out what matters to you in life and, hopefully, you're finding someone great to spend your life with," says Joe. "And you know, when you're starting out, a couple of great Italian recipes can help."

"In Italy, when you're a young couple, you have a lot of people helping you," adds Vittorio. "You learn to cook everything from scratch. You learn sauce from one person, bread from another. Sometimes, especially when you're starting out, you need to watch your money, what you spend on the food you make. If you have a few good vegetables, good olive oil, good bread—that's all it really takes for good living. And a little electricity. When you marry for love, if you know how to cook a little, to keep your wife happy, to keep your husband happy, that's a good thing."

Over the years, we've been the site for hundreds of marriage proposals, countless rehearsal dinners and dozens of weddings—some we knew were coming, some we didn't. Stories abound of finding a judge on the spot and hosting a spontaneous wedding in the Pope's Room. Many couples have made our restaurants an important part of their lives, and that's just one reason we say, "At Buca di Beppo, famiglia begins with two!"

Joe's parents on
their wedding day.

Sweetheart Tortellini

(Tortellini Innamorati)

1/4 cup olive oil

2 ounces shiitake or oyster mushrooms, sliced

1 cup Alfredo Sauce
  (see recipe on page 50)

1/2 cup frozen peas

3 ounces prosciutto, thinly sliced
  and julienned

10 ounces fresh meat tortellini

1/2 cup grated Parmigiano-Reggiano cheese

2 tablespoons finely diced red bell pepper

2 tomato roses, made from fresh tomatoes
  (see note)

* * * * *

In a small sauté pan, heat the olive oil over medium-high heat and sauté the mushrooms until light brown. Set aside. In a large sauté pan, heat the Alfredo Sauce over low heat. When hot add the mushrooms, peas and prosciutto. Keep warm.

In a large pan, bring water to a boil and add the meat tortellini; cook until al dente, strain, add to the sauce and toss well. Divide the tortellini into two serving bowls; sprinkle first with cheese and then diced red pepper. Garnish with tomato roses and serve.

* * * * *

Note: To make tomato roses, use a sharp paring knife to cut off the tomato skin in a long ribbon. Roll up the long piece of tomato skin into the shape of a rose.

Serves 2.

Angel Hair Pasta with Shrimp

(Capellini con Gamberetti)

1/4 cup olive oil

1 tablespoon chopped garlic

1/2 pound medium shrimp,
   peeled and deveined

1 cup fresh cherry tomatoes,
   halved

Salt to taste

Pepper to taste

1/2 pound angel hair pasta

1 1/2 tablespoons chopped
   fresh basil

In a medium saucepan, heat the olive oil over medium-high heat and sauté the garlic until it is light brown. Add the shrimp and cook for about 2 minutes. Add the tomatoes, salt and pepper, and cook over low heat for 4 to 5 minutes.

While the sauce is cooking, bring a pot of water to a boil and add the pasta, cooking until al dente. Make sure to stir the pasta so that it does not stick together. Drain the pasta and add the sauce. Toss well, garnish with fresh basil and serve.

For best flavor, do not use any grated cheese on this dish.

Serves 2.

Omelet with Escarole and Cheese
(Frittata con Escarole e Formaggio)

1 pound escarole (greens only)
2 tablespoons olive oil
4 ounces oyster mushrooms
1/2 cup chopped red onion
1 tablespoon chopped garlic
8 large eggs, beaten
1/4 cup grated Pecorino Romano cheese
1/4 cup grated provolone cheese
Salt to taste
Pepper to taste

* * * * *

In a large pot of boiling water, cook the escarole, drain and place in cold water. Squeeze the escarole dry, chop into 1-inch pieces and set aside.

In a 12-inch nonstick skillet, heat the olive oil over medium heat. Add the mushrooms, onion and garlic. Cook, stirring until soft and brown, approximately 5 minutes.

In a mixing bowl, combine the eggs, escarole, cheeses, salt and pepper. Mix well. Pour the egg mixture into the skillet, incorporate the egg mixture with the vegetables and cook until the bottom has set and is firm, approximately 5 minutes. Holding a flat plate over the skillet, turn the frittata over onto its other side and slide back into the skillet. Cook an additional 5 minutes or until the frittata is firm and lightly brown.

Divide the frittata and serve.

Serves 4.

Baked Pasta
(Macaroni al Forno)

1 pound rigatoni, penne or other
  tube-shaped pasta
3 cups Marinara Sauce
  (see recipe on page 44), warmed
2 (6-ounce) skinless, boneless chicken
  breasts, cooked and diced
2 ounces pepperoni, thinly sliced
2 ounces mortadella cheese, sliced in
  2-by-2-inch squares
4 ounces feta cheese, grated
3 ounces Pecorino Romano cheese, grated
4 eggs, hard-boiled and quartered

Preheat the oven to 400 degrees.

In a large pot of boiling water, cook the pasta until al dente, drain and place in a large mixing bowl. Add the warm Marinara Sauce and mix well so that the pasta does not stick together. Add the cooked chicken breast, pepperoni, mortadella cheese and feta cheese, then toss the ingredients together. Place the mixture in a large, oiled baking dish. Sprinkle the Romano cheese evenly over the ingredients and place the hard-boiled egg quarters on top. Bake 10 to 15 minutes or until lightly browned.

Serves 6.

Nick Iammarino's sisters and brother pose with relatives for a family portrait.

Melted Mozzarella Sandwich

(Mozzarella in Carrozza)

4 large slices Italian bread
1 large ball fresh mozzarella
   cheese, sliced 1/8-inch thick
3 ounces prosciutto, thinly sliced
1 to 2 teaspoons chopped fresh sage
1/2 cup olive oil
1/2 cup flour
2 eggs, beaten
3/4 cup Italian-style bread crumbs
2 cups Marinara Sauce
   (see recipe on page 44)

Preheat oven to 400 degrees.
On a bread slice, evenly lay a quarter
of the cheese. Cover cheese with half of
the prosciutto. Sprinkle with half
of the fresh sage. Add a second
layer of cheese. Top with another
slice of bread, sandwich style.
Repeat process for second sandwich.
In a large sauté pan, heat the olive
oil over medium heat until hot. Coat
each sandwich in flour, then add in
the eggs and the bread crumbs.
Fry sandwiches until light brown
on both sides. Bake in the oven
for approximately 5 minutes,
or until cheese is melted. Cut
each sandwich in half and serve
on a plate with a cup of hot
Marinara Sauce for each.

Serves 2.

Potato Tart Apulian Style
(Focaccia Pugliese con Patate)

1/2 pound potatoes
4 slices bacon, cooked crisp and chopped
1/2 cup grated Parmigiano-Reggiano cheese
1/4 cup julienned red onions
Salt to taste
Pepper to taste
1 whole egg
1 egg yolk
1/4 cup white wine
1 tablespoon cap[...]

* * *

Prehea[...]
Wash an[...]

potatoes using the large side of a cheese grater. Put the potato pieces in a bowl of cold water and rinse them to remove the extra starch. Pat the pieces dry. In a small bowl, mix the potatoes with the bacon; add the cheese, onion, salt and pepper. Beat the egg and egg yolk together with the wine, add to the potatoes and mix well. Butter a shallow (1-inch-deep) 10-[...]ch round baking dish or 10-inch tart pan with [...]ovable bottom, then pour the potato-egg [...]re into the dish. Top with capers. Put the [...]tart in the oven and cook until the surface [...]nd golden, approximately 1 hour.

[...] a delicious supper dish and [...]d with a fresh green salad.

Speak Italian in 10 minutes or less!
HANDY WALLET SIZE FOR YOUR CONVENIENCE!

Hello -- Ciao!
Thank you -- Grazie!
You're welcome -- Prego!
Please -- Per favore
Excuse me -- Scusi
Beautiful -- Bellissimo
Cute -- Bellino
Delicious -- Buonissimo
Happy Birthday -- Buon compleanno!
Fantastic -- Fantastico!
Goodbye -- Arrivederci!
A little more, please -- Ancora un po, per favore
This is the best food I've ever tasted in my life -- Questo è il migliore cibo che abbia mai assaggiato
I would like a bottle of wine -- Desidero una bottiglia di vino

Orecchiette Pasta Salad with Vegetables
(Insalata di Orecchiette con Verdura)

2 small zucchini
2 small carrots
1/4 pound escarole
4 medium-size ripe tomatoes
1 medium cucumber
1 pound orecchiette
1 teaspoon chopped garlic
3 tablespoons chopped fresh basil
1/4 pound feta cheese, crumbled
1/2 cup extra-virgin olive oil
1/4 cup balsamic vinegar
Salt to taste
Pepper to taste

* * * * *

Wash and dice zucchini and carrots, and then scald in boiling water until tender. Drain,

cool and set aside. Wash and drain the escarole. Coarsely chop it and set aside. Dice the tomatoes and place them in a sieve to drain some of the juice; set aside. Wash the cucumber, pat dry and dice (leaving the skin on); set aside.

Cook the pasta in boiling water until al dente. Refresh under cold water. Drain thoroughly.

In a large bowl, mix the orecchiette with the cucumber, tomatoes, carrots, zucchini, escarole, garlic, basil and cheese. Toss with the olive oil, balsamic vinegar, salt and pepper. Chill in refrigerator, and serve cold in a pasta bowl.

Serves 4.

Vieri is not only a master winemaker, he is also a skilled olive oil maker. Here he describes the traditional method of making olive oil.

This is the most traditional Southern Italian soup. It is served on wedding days to bring happiness, love and health to the newlyweds, but it's easy enough to serve any day.

Wedding Soup

(Zuppa Maritata)

4 ounces bulk Italian sausage

8 cups chicken stock

1 (6-ounce) skinless,
   boneless chicken breast,
   diced into 1-inch pieces

1 cup chopped escarole

Salt to taste

Pepper to taste

1 cup pastina (confetti-shaped pasta)

2 eggs, lightly beaten

1 ounce grated Pecorino Romano cheese

2 tablespoons chopped red bell pepper

Brown the sausage, let it cool, then chop and set aside. In a large saucepan, bring the chicken stock to a boil, add the chicken and sausage, and simmer over low heat for 15 minutes. Add the escarole, salt and pepper. In a pot of boiling water, cook the pastina until al dente, drain and add to the soup. Very slowly, pour the eggs in a stream into the soup, mixing well (the eggs should form fine threads). Remove from the heat. Place the soup in a large serving bowl and garnish with cheese and diced red peppers.

Serves 4.

Joe's mother and father (far right) pose for a family photo at one of their many get-togethers.

Celebrations!

At Buca di Beppo, we're famous for having big tables, big platters and a big, big ability to accommodate big groups. Why do we do it? It's not just our big hearts: at Buca di Beppo, our emotional roots are planted in the Italian and Italian-American experiences, where generations live in the same town and neighbors celebrate feasts, holidays and plain old Sundays all together. At the Italian table, you never know how many people are going to show up for supper, so you just make plenty of extra food and pull up all the available chairs and stools.

* "For Italians, food sets the table for community," explains Joe. "At Buca di Beppo, we're not just serving great food, we're also serving the experience of being a part of the Italian table—the welcome, the wonder. When you see one of our huge platters hit the table, part of you goes, 'Oh, wow!' You can't believe it. It's like you're a kid in your family's kitchen: there's more food than you can imagine and everything's taken care of.

* "I remember when I was growing up and my grandfather would make braciola on Sundays—my favorite. (You take flank or round steak and pound it till it's tender, spread it with a paste of eggs and Parmesan cheese, roll it up and tie it with string, sear it in a pan and then simmer it in tomato sauce.) We would go to a later mass at church, and while you were in the house in the morning you'd smell everything—and you'd be thinking about it when you went to church. Let's just say you did not waste any time getting home. You ran. Monday lunches were the best, because you'd have leftovers from Sunday. By the time Wednesday rolled around and you were back to eating peanut butter and jelly, you were depressed. Sometimes I'll see somebody carrying a bag out of Buca di Beppo after dinner and I'll think, Monday lunch. That's living." ✳

Se non sopporta il calore

At the Kitchen Table at Buca di Beppo.

✳ ✳

Not a night goes by at a Buca di Beppo when someone doesn't ask to take home one of our signature wicker-wrapped wine bottles. Yes, they make great candleholders, but we like to think it's more than that. While it's true our wine list covers almost all of the entire Italian peninsula and ranges in price from very affordable rosé to fancy vintage Amarone, that wicker bottle captures something essential about the Southern Italian immigrant experience of abundance, exuberance and informality.

The red wine in that classic bottle is Chianti, the classic table wine of the Italian region of Tuscany. If you order a bottle of Chianti, you're participating in one of the world's oldest food traditions. Some historians say vineyards have existed in the Tuscan hills since the time of the ancient Greeks, forming in time the all-important Italian dietary trinity of wheat, olive

oil and wine. The first records of official wine shops date to before the Middle Ages. Some of the first laws stated that wine couldn't be sold to children under 15 and forbade shops from harboring ruffians! One early member of the Italian wine guilds came from the Antinori family. A careful reader will note that Antinori wines are on our wine list even today; order a bottle and you'll partake in a nearly 800-year tradition of Italian winemaking. But we serve the wines in casual juice glasses. Why? Because at Buca di Beppo, we believe that wine should never be uppity.

It's the Italian immigrant philosophy: it's not about having fancy stemware; it's about having glasses that are functional and

---

Opposite page: The Buca di Beppo Wicker Basket Bianco earns Vieri's seal of approval and ours! This page: A little piggy goes to an Italian market.

✳ ✳ ✳ ✳ ✳ ✳ ✳ ✳ ✳   ✳ ✳ ✳ ✳ ✳ ✳ ✳ ✳ ✳

✳ ✳

wine that's approachable.

That's also why we commissioned a wine we are terrifically proud of, our Wicker Basket Bianco, a blend made just for Buca di Beppo by Vieri Salvadori, master vinter, at La Tancia vineyard in Italy. Our Wicker Basket Bianco is a special blend made from Chardonnay grapes and from Malvasia grapes, which have a fruity scent and great body. The resulting wine is crisp and dry but offers a lovely smell, making it the perfect wine to go with a variety of our dishes, such as our Chicken with Lemon or Macaroni Rosa.

"When I was growing up we actually would squeeze wine with our feet," remembers Vittorio. "You get all the grapes, put them together in a big wooden chest, and get in there and jump and jump and jump. You strain out the juice and make the wine. Whenever my father would have a friend over, he'd offer him a little homemade wine. At the end of a meal at Buca di Beppo, you might look around and see you have a glass of wine and an espresso at the same time. Now you're really Italian! Sometimes I have such a long day—I go on television in the morning, teach a class all day, am in the restaurant cooking at night—but I might not even be tired! I say it's my mother's fault: when I was born she must have mixed up the baby bottles and, instead of milk, I got a bottle of homemade wine and a bottle of espresso, and I haven't unwound since." ✳

The photo shows the view from La Tancia, a *fattoria* (or winery) located in the Italy's Tuscan countryside, just kilometers outside of Florence. Vieri calls the picture perfect location "home." His family has held this land since 1843. This beautiful winery is where our Chianti Riserva and Wicker Basket Bianco are made. Opposite page: This cart, overloaded with wicker basket-covered wine bottles shows how wine used to be transported.

✳ ✳

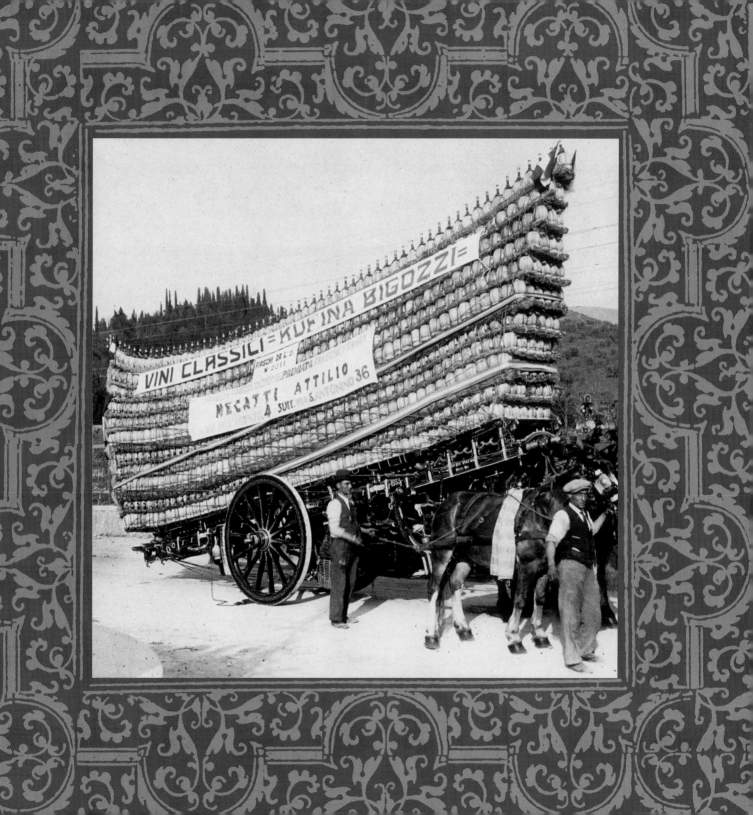

✳ ✳

"My father used to make large amounts of this recipe, which can be served over fried escarole, homemade gnocchi or pasta (leftovers reheat great). This dish is especially common on Easter and Christmas Eve." —Vittorio

Sicilian Lamb Stew
(Agnello alla Siciliana)

2 pounds leg of lamb, cubed into 1-inch pieces
6 tablespoons olive oil
3 tablespoons flour
1 cup water
1 (28-ounce) can of crushed tomatoes
Salt to taste
1 large eggplant, skin on, cubed into
    1/2-inch pieces
1 pound russet potatoes, peeled and cubed
    into 1/2-inch pieces
1 large red onion, chopped into 1/2-inch pieces
1/2 pound fresh mushrooms, quartered
2 tablespoons chopped fresh sage
Pepper to taste

* * * * *

In a large braising pan, brown the meat in 2 tablespoons of the olive oil over medium heat until its moisture has evaporated. Add the flour and stir until absorbed. Add the water, tomatoes and salt. Cook over medium heat until meat is tender, about 1 hour.

Place the eggplant in a bowl, sprinkle with salt and let stand for 30 minutes. Pat eggplant dry, and set aside.

In a pot of boiling water, cook the potatoes until soft. Drain and set aside.

In a large sauté pan, heat the remaining olive oil. Sauté onion, mushrooms and eggplant until brown and tender. Set aside. When the meat stew is thick and tender, add the potatoes, vegetables, fresh sage and pepper. Cook for about 5 minutes. Serve hot.

Serves 4.

✳ ✳ ✳ ✳ ✳ ✳ ✳ ✳ ✳ ✳ ✳   ✳ ✳ ✳ ✳ ✳ ✳ ✳ ✳ ✳ ✳ ✳

✳ ✳

Grandpa's Salt Cod
(Baccalà del Nonno Skipeci)

4 6-ounce dry salt cod fillets
  (or 1-pound box frozen salt cod)
1/2 cup calamata olives, pitted and halved
1/2 cup green olives, pitted and halved
1/4 cup chopped red onion
3/4 cup plus 3 tablespoons olive oil
1/2 cup flour
1 (28-ounce) can chopped tomatoes
1/2 cup white wine
2 tablespoons dried oregano
1/4 cup fresh lemon juice
Salt to taste
1 pound russet potatoes, peeled and
  cut into wedges
4 lemon wedges

* * * * *

Place the salt cod in a large plastic container and cover with fresh water. Let the cod soak, changing water every 4 to 6 hours, until it is soft and water isn't too salty. In a large braising pan, sauté the olives and onion in 3 tablespoons of olive oil over medium heat. Set aside. Dust cod pieces in flour and sauté in 3/4 cup of olive oil until both sides are brown, about 4 minutes per side. Set aside fish; discard the frying oil.

In a mixing bowl, make a cold sauce by combining the tomatoes, wine, oregano, lemon juice, salt, olives and onion. Add sauce to braising pan. Over medium heat, bring the sauce to a boil. Add browned cod. Reduce heat to low and cook covered for 30 minutes, until fish is tender.

Meanwhile, boil the potato wedges until al dente. Drain and add potatoes to the cod about 10 minutes before it is done cooking.

Gently place the cod on a large serving platter. Pour the sauce over the fish and arrange the potatoes around the fish. Garnish with lemon wedges.

Serves 4.

✳ ✳

Friends of Buca di Beppo celebrate their 25th wedding anniversary at the restaurant.

✳ ✳

"This dish used to be one of my father's favorites. In Southern Italy, Sunday is family day. After church, friends and family dine together and enjoy great dishes of pasta and meat served together for sharing." —Vittorio

Sunday Rolled Stuffed Beef
(Braciola della Domenica)

1 cup dry Italian-style bread crumbs
1/4 cup chopped garlic
3 ounces Pecorino Romano cheese, grated
3 tablespoons chopped Italian parsley
2 eggs
1 pound flank steak
4 hard-boiled eggs
6 cups Marinara Sauce (see recipe on page 44)
1/2 cup heavy cream
1 pound cavatelli

* * * * *

To make the stuffing, mix the bread crumbs, garlic, cheese, parsley and eggs in a bowl. Set aside.
Pound the flank steak until it is 1/4-inch thick. Flatten the stuffing onto the middle of the steak, from end to end. Lay the whole hard-boiled eggs over the stuffing, roll up the steak like a salami and secure with string. Set aside.

In a large pan, bring the Marinara Sauce to a boil, lower the heat, and add the braciola, covering it in sauce. Cook with lid on for 1 hour or until the sauce is thick, stirring regularly. Remove the braciola and set aside. Add the cream to the sauce and keep warm over very low heat.

Cook pasta until al dente, drain and toss with the sauce. Place pasta on a large platter. Remove the string from the braciola. Slice braciola into 1-inch-thick pieces, arrange over pasta and serve.

Serves 4.

✳ ✳ ✳ ✳ ✳ ✳ ✳ ✳ ✳ ✳ ✳ ✳   ✳ ✳ ✳ ✳ ✳ ✳ ✳ ✳ ✳ ✳ ✳ ✳

✳ ✳

Cornish Game Hens with Spinach Sauce
(Galletto con Salsa di Spinaci)

4 1-pound Cornish game hens
1 cup olive oil
1 tablespoon crushed red pepper flakes
2 tablespoons chopped, fresh rosemary
1 tablespoon dried oregano
Salt to taste
Spinach Sauce
  (see recipe on page 125)

* * * * *

Split open the back of each Cornish game hen with a sharp knife or poultry shears. Remove the giblets, rinse under cold water and pat dry with paper towels. Flatten, leaving hens in one piece.

Place olive oil, crushed red pepper flakes, rosemary, oregano and salt in a large bowl and mix well. Add hens to the mixture and marinate for approximately 2 hours, turning the hens from time to time.

Preheat oven to 350 degrees. Place the hens on a large sheet pan, skin side down. Spoon some of the marinade over the hens. Bake for approximately 45 minutes, turn the hens skin side up, and continue baking for another 30 minutes, or until the meat is done and skin is golden brown and crisp.

Remove the hens from the oven, place on serving dishes and top with Spinach Sauce. Serve hot.

Serves 4.

This recipe doubles or even quadruples well, and is perfect for larger dinner parties.

✳ ✳ ✳ ✳ ✳ ✳ ✳ ✳ ✳ ✳ ✳   ✳ ✳ ✳ ✳ ✳ ✳ ✳ ✳ ✳ ✳ ✳

✳✳✳✳✳✳✳✳✳✳✳✳✳✳✳✳✳✳✳✳✳✳✳✳✳✳✳✳✳

Lasagne Casserole

(Lasagne Pasticciata)

2 large eggplants, sliced 1/8-inch thick

Salt to taste

1 cup olive oil

2 pounds potatoes, peeled and
   sliced 1/8-inch thick

8 (5-by-8-inch) fresh pasta sheets

4 cups Tomato Meat Sauce
   (see recipe on page 49)

2 cups Béchamel Sauce
   (see recipe on page 125)

4 ounces grated Pecorino
   Romano cheese

* * * * *

Preheat oven to 350 degrees.
Sprinkle sliced eggplants with salt.
Let rest 30 minutes, then drain off any
liquid and pat dry. Fry eggplant in
olive oil until brown on both sides
and set aside. Blanch potatoes and
set aside. Lightly coat the bottom of
a 9-by-13-inch baking dish with olive
oil, spread out one fresh pasta sheet
and coat evenly with Tomato Meat
Sauce. Place one layer of eggplant
over the meat sauce and top eggplant
with a layer of potatoes. Spread a
layer of Béchamel Sauce evenly over
the potatoes and top with cheese.
Repeat the process until all of the
ingredients are used (three to four
layers). Finish with a layer of
Béchamel Sauce and cheese. Cover
the pan with aluminum foil and bake
for about 1 1/2 hours. Remove the
foil and cook an additional 15
minutes. Let the lasagne stand at
room temperature for approximately
30 minutes. Cut the lasagna into
4-by-4-inch squares and serve.

Serves 6.

✳✳✳✳✳✳✳✳✳✳✳✳   ✳✳✳✳✳✳✳✳✳✳✳✳

✳ ✳

Béchamel Sauce

1/2 cup butter
1/2 cup flour
4 cups milk, scalded
1 teaspoon salt
1 teaspoon pepper
Pinch of nutmeg

* * * * *

In a large saucepan over medium heat, melt the butter and slowly mix in the flour, cooking for about 2 to 3 minutes until it forms a light golden brown paste, called a roux. Add the hot milk, about 1/4 cup at a time, whisking well to whip out any lumps. Continue until milk has all been added, then add the salt, pepper and nutmeg, and cook for about 10 minutes, stirring often, until the sauce has thickened. Cool in the refrigerator until ready to use.

Makes 8 cups.

Spinach Sauce

1 quart heavy cream
4 ounces garlic cloves, sliced
1 pound frozen spinach, drained well
  and chopped
2 teaspoons salt
2 teaspoons pepper
2 ounces butter

* * * * *

In a small saucepan, bring the cream to a simmer over medium-low heat. Add the garlic. Cook until the cream is reduced by half. Add the spinach, salt and pepper, and heat through, cooking for approximately 5 minutes.

Remove sauce from the heat and add butter. Mix well until the sauce has thickened. If you prefer a smoother sauce, purée in a blender or food processor.

Makes 4 cups.

✳ ✳ ✳ ✳ ✳ ✳ ✳ ✳ ✳ ✳ ✳   ✳ ✳ ✳ ✳ ✳ ✳ ✳ ✳ ✳ ✳ ✳

✳ ✳

Breaded Veal with Fennel
(Vitello Impanato al Finocchio)

2 tablespoons fennel seeds
2 cups dry Italian-style bread crumbs
1 cup flour
4 large eggs, beaten
8 3-ounce veal scaloppini, thinly pounded
Salt to taste
Pepper to taste
1/2 cup olive oil
2 cups Marinara Sauce
   (see recipe on page 44), warm
1 pound Roma tomatoes, diced
   into 1/4-inch pieces
10 ounces provolone cheese,
   cubed into 1/4-inch pieces

* * * * *

Preheat oven to 350 degrees.

Place fennel seeds on a baking sheet and bake until toasted, about 10 minutes. Cool and finely chop in a spice grinder or with a mortar and pestle. In a mixing bowl, mix the bread crumbs with the fennel seeds. Set aside 1 tablespoon of the mixture.

Place the flour, beaten eggs and crumb mixture in three separate shallow pans. Sprinkle the veal with salt and pepper. Coat veal in flour, then eggs and then bread crumbs. Pat veal well to remove excess bread crumbs. In a large sauté pan over medium-high heat, sauté each scaloppini in batches in the olive oil until light brown on both sides.

Place cooked veal on a large baking sheet and cover with large spoonfuls of Marinara Sauce. Top evenly with the tomatoes and cheese.

Bake veal until cheese is melted, about 12 minutes. Cover the bottom of a large serving dish with the remaining sauce; place the veal on the sauce and sprinkle with reserved crumb mixture. Serve hot.

Serves 4.

✳ ✳ ✳ ✳ ✳ ✳ ✳ ✳ ✳ ✳ ✳ ✳   ✳ ✳ ✳ ✳ ✳ ✳ ✳ ✳ ✳ ✳ ✳ ✳

✳✳✳✳✳✳✳✳✳✳✳✳✳✳✳✳✳✳✳✳✳✳✳✳✳✳✳✳✳✳

Potato Dumplings with Peas and Gorgonzola
(Gnocchi con Gorgonzola e Piselli)

1 pound russet potatoes

1 egg, lightly beaten

Salt to taste

Pepper to taste

2/3 cup flour

1 batch Gorgonzola Sauce
   (see recipe page 129)

Grated Parmigiano-Reggiano cheese
   for dusting

4 ounces fresh or frozen peas

* * * * *

Cook the potatoes in boiling water until tender. Drain and peel the potatoes.

Mash the potatoes, then add the eggs, salt and pepper. On a cutting board, turn out the potato mixture. Gently knead in enough flour to form a soft, smooth dough. Divide into 3 equal portions, each the size of a baseball. Roll each ball in flour, then roll each ball into a 3/4-inch-thick rope. Cut each rope into 20 pieces, 3/4-inch wide. Dust each gnocchi with flour on each side. In a large pot of boiling water, cook the gnocchi in small batches (about 10 at a time) until they rise to the surface.

Mix peas (thaw beforehand, if frozen) into the Gorgonzola Sauce. Divide the sauce onto serving plates, then drain gnocchi and place equal amounts on top of the sauce on each plate. Dust with cheese and serve.

Serves 4.

✳✳✳✳✳✳✳✳✳✳✳   ✳✳✳✳✳✳✳✳✳✳✳

✳✳✳✳✳✳✳✳✳✳✳✳✳✳✳✳✳✳✳✳✳✳✳✳✳✳✳✳✳

Gorgonzola is a sweet, creamy, buttery blue cheese made from cow's milk. Try to avoid substituting an aged, crumbly blue cheese for sweet (dolce) Gorgonzola, because it might overpower the recipe.

Gorgonzola Sauce

1 tablespoon chopped shallots

2 tablespoons unsalted butter

1 cup dry white wine

1 quart heavy cream

8 ounces Gorgonzola cheese, crumbled

1/2 cup chopped parsley

Salt to taste

Pepper to taste

In a saucepan over medium heat, sauté the shallots in the butter until translucent, about 5 minutes. Add the wine and cook until the wine has evaporated. Add the cream and cheese. Continue cooking until the sauce has reduced by a third. Mix in the parsley, salt and pepper.

Makes 4 cups.

✳✳✳✳✳✳✳✳✳✳✳✳ ✳✳✳✳✳✳✳✳✳✳✳✳

✳ ✳

"Siracusa is a city in Sicily where the swordfish caught near this beautiful Mediterranean island is the most popular of all fish. The Sicilians cook swordfish in many different ways. This is one of my favorites because the light sauce does not overpower the freshness or moistness of the fish." —Vittorio

Swordfish Siracusa-Style
(Pesce Spada Siracusa)

4 8-ounce swordfish steaks
Salt to taste
Pepper to taste
1/4 cup olive oil
2 teaspoons chopped garlic
1/4 cup white wine
1 teaspoon dried oregano
1/4 cup fresh lemon juice
6 ounces whole calamata olives,
  pitted and halved
1/4 cup capers
2 bay leaves
2 medium Roma tomatoes,
  quartered and seeded

Place the swordfish, seasoned with salt and pepper, in a deep sauté pan. In a large bowl, make a cold sauce with the remaining ingredients. Mix well. Pour sauce over the swordfish, and cook over medium-high heat for approximately 20 minutes, until the swordfish is cooked and the sauce is reduced by half. Do not stir the sauce or the swordfish will break. Gently, using a spatula, place the swordfish on a serving platter, spoon the sauce over the swordfish and serve immediately.

Serves 4.

✳ ✳ ✳ ✳ ✳ ✳ ✳ ✳ ✳ ✳ ✳ ✳   ✳ ✳ ✳ ✳ ✳ ✳ ✳ ✳ ✳ ✳ ✳ ✳

La Dolce Vita

DESSERTS

Puff Pastry Cake with Fresh Figs

Mascarpone and Espresso Cake

Warm Marsala Wine Custard

Amaretti with Flavored Mascarpone

Sweet Layer Dessert

Sicilian Cannoli

Fried Doughnuts Filled with Pastry Cream

Poached Pears with Honey Sauce

Ricotta Cheesecake

Filled Holiday Crêpes

Neapolitan Cookies

In Italy, most Italians get their desserts from the neighborhood pastry shop, the *pasticceria*. Homemade desserts are usually reserved for special occasions such as a birthday or a feast-day celebration. ✳ "My father used to make 'bombolini,' little fried desserts filled with pastry cream, for my sister Maria. They were her very favorite," remembers Vittorio. "But desserts were not something you made every single day. My grandfather made a simple dessert with amaretti every Sunday, but for every day? No. Mostly you stop at a pasticceria and get some nice little treats: 'cannolis,' little cookies, pastries filled with chocolate custard. What you might do is finish up your meal with a little 'limoncello.' "

✳ Limoncello is a lemon-infused liqueur with which Italians toast the end of a meal. It's considered a *digestivo*, something to help you digest your food. At Buca di Beppo we make our limoncello from scratch. It is made from the yellow rind of a lemon, which is soaked in high-proof alcohol for several weeks; the liqueur is combined with simple sugar syrup to create an intense beverage that is served ice-cold.

✳ "That's one of the great things about Italian culture," muses Vittorio. "Every minute of the day there's some tradition you can do. Wake up, boom—espresso. Boom—it's 11 o'clock, time for a little something to stimulate the appetite for lunch, an *aperitivo*, like Campari. Maybe you have some little snacks to start. Boom—lunch. Maybe you work a little bit. Now it's time for an afternoon coffee—boom, you're back at the espresso bar. Maybe get a little 'gelato.' At 6, another aperitivo, then dinner, a little digestivo. Now it's late, boom—out to the 'piazza.' You sit at a café on the sidewalk, have a little espresso, maybe another digestivo, a limoncello maybe. Then you go to bed, and the good news is you can start all over in the morning!" ✖

Puff Pastry Cake with Fresh Figs

(Sfoglia con Fichi)

1 8-by-10-inch sheet of
   puff pastry
8 ounces mascarpone cheese
1/4 cup sugar
2 pints fresh black figs
1 loaf of pound cake
1 cup apricot glaze
   (or strained apricot jam)
1/4 cup water
1/4 cup sambuca
1 pint heavy cream, whipped

* * * * *

Preheat the oven to 425 degrees. Place the puff pastry on a sheet pan lined with parchment paper. Prick pastry so it doesn't puff too much, then cook until it is light brown, approximately 20 minutes. Set aside to cool on a rack.

Mix the cheese with the sugar and set aside. Wash the figs, pat dry, cut into 1/8-inch-thick slices and set aside.

Cut the pound cake lengthwise into 4 equal parts and set aside.

Pour the apricot glaze into a small saucepan and heat until melted. Keep warm.

Mix the water and sambuca and set aside.

Place the puff pastry on a small sheet pan and cover it evenly with the pound cake. Brush the cake with the sambuca mix, soaking the cake. With a spatula, spread the mascarpone mix evenly over the pound cake. Place the sliced figs over the mascarpone layer evenly to cover the bottom. Brush the top of the fresh figs with the warm apricot glaze. Refrigerate the cake until ready to serve. To serve, cut into square pieces and top with the whipped cream.

Serves 8.

Mascarpone and Espresso Cake
(Tiramisu)

3 egg yolks
5 tablespoons sugar
1 pound mascarpone cheese
1 cup espresso
3 ounces brandy
3 dozen lady fingers
1 tablespoon cocoa powder
3 ounces crushed biscotti

* * * * *

 raw egg In a mixing bowl, beat the egg yolks with the sugar. Add the cheese and mix well. In another bowl, mix together the espresso and brandy.

Soak 1 lady finger in the brandy-espresso mixture at a time; let excess drip off and place in a deep serving dish. Top evenly with the mascarpone mix. Repeat the process until all of the lady fingers and mascarpone mix have been used. Sprinkle with cocoa powder and top with biscotti. Refrigerate for about 2 hours. For best results, make the tiramisu 4 hours prior to serving and refrigerate.

Serves 6.

Note: Be aware that any recipe that calls for uncooked eggs means bacteria could be present.

Warm Marsala Wine Custard
(Zabagione)

2 cups dry Marsala wine
1 cup sugar
1/4 cup flour
15 egg yolks

* * * * *

In a saucepan, heat the wine to 150 degrees; set aside. In a large metal mixing bowl, combine the sugar, flour and egg yolks, and mix well to avoid lumps. Add the wine slowly. Place the bowl over low heat and, whisking constantly, cook the custard until it is thick. Remove from heat.

Serve warm or refrigerate and serve cold.

Makes 6 cups.

Warm Marsala Wine Custard (see recipe on page 137), shown here topped over fresh berries.

"This rich and creamy mascarpone dessert doesn't require cooking.
My Grandpa Francesco used to make this dessert for my family
every Sunday as I was growing up." —Vittorio

Amaretti with Flavored Mascarpone

(Coppa di Francesco)

36 large amaretti cookies
1/4 cup rum
1/4 cup anise-flavored liqueur
4 eggs
1/2 cup sugar
1 pound mascarpone cheese, softened
1 cup heavy cream, whipped
3 ounces chocolate shavings

* * * * *

Divide cookies among 6 dessert bowls.
Mix the rum and the liqueur, then
drizzle the mixture over the cookies.

Whip the eggs and sugar in a medium
bowl until light in color. Add the cheese
and beat until smooth and creamy. Spoon
the mascarpone mixture evenly into each
dessert bowl. Cover with plastic wrap
and refrigerate until firm, approximately
2 hours. (You can make this dish ahead
of time and refrigerate it overnight.) Put
a dollop of whipped cream on each
serving and sprinkle with chocolate
shavings just prior to serving.

Serves 6.

Note: Be aware that any recipe
that calls for uncooked eggs means
bacteria could be present.

Sweet Layer Dessert
(Dolce Zuppa Inglese)

2 loaves of pound cake
1/2 cup Grand Marnier
2 cups Vanilla Custard
  (recipe follows)
1/2 pound semisweet
  chocolate, chopped
1 cup maraschino cherries, chopped
2 cups Chocolate Custard
  (recipe follows)
8 ounces nougat with nuts, chopped
1 pint whipping cream

Chocolate and Vanilla Custard
1 quart milk
1 cup sugar
1 teaspoon vanilla
2 ounces flour
10 egg yolks
4 ounces semisweet chocolate, chopped

* * * * *

Custard:
In a small saucepan, combine the milk and sugar. Place over medium heat and bring to a boil. In a mixing bowl, combine the vanilla, flour and egg yolks, and whip until it thickens. Pour the hot milk into the egg mixture. Whip into a smooth custard. Pour

the custard back into the saucepan and, over medium heat, cook the custard, continuing to stir, until it is thickened. Divide the custard into two bowls or pans. Add chopped semisweet chocolate to one bowl and whip until all of the chocolate is incorporated. Refrigerate both bowls of custard until cool.

Dessert:

Slice the pound cake into pieces 1/4-inch thick and 4-by-4-inches wide and lay a few pieces on the bottom of a crystal or ceramic bowl. Brush the pound cake with Grand Marnier, evenly spread with vanilla custard, and

sprinkle with some of the chopped chocolate, cherries and nougat. Add another layer of pound cake soaked with Grand Marnier, evenly spread with chocolate custard, and sprinkle with chopped chocolate and cherries. Repeat the process until a few layers are formed. Refrigerate. Before serving, whip the cream until stiff. Place a large spoonful of Zuppa Inglese on a dessert plate and garnish with whipped cream.

For best results, make this dessert at least 2 hours before serving.

Serves 6 to 8.

Italian ricotta is usually made from sheep or water buffalo's milk,
and has a nutty taste; American ricotta is made from cow's milk,
and is sweeter and milder. Either will work for this recipe,
but they create very different results!

Sicilian Cannoli

(Cannoli Taormina)

3 cups ricotta cheese

1/2 cup granulated sugar

4 ounces chocolate, chopped

2 ounces plain, roasted pistachio nuts,
 chopped

6 tablespoons Frangelico

12 cannoli shells

1 cup Chocolate Custard
 (see recipe on page 140)

2 tablespoons powdered sugar

Place the cheese, sugar, chopped chocolate, pistachio nuts and Frangelico in a large bowl and mix well. Spread the chocolate custard over the bottom of a large serving platter. With a tipless pastry bag, fill the cannoli shells. Place the cannolis on the chocolate custard, sprinkle with powdered sugar and serve.

Serves 6.

142

"Bombolini con Crema is my sister Maria's favorite. My father made it for her frequently. Throughout Southern Italy these are served often on Halloween and at the Feast of San Joseph." —Vittorio

Fried Doughnuts Filled with Pastry Cream
(Bombolini con Crema)

1 cup whole milk
1/2 cup butter
Pinch of salt
1 teaspoon sugar
1 1/2 cups flour
4 eggs
3 1/4 cups olive oil
1/2 batch Pastry Cream
  (recipe follows)
2 cups powdered sugar

In a medium saucepan, bring milk, butter, salt and sugar to a boil. Remove pan from the heat and mix in the flour. Return to low heat and mix until batter pulls away from the sides of the pan. Place batter in an electric mixing bowl and using a paddle attachment, on low speed, mix until dough cools to 130 degrees. Add the eggs one at a time, until all are incorporated.

In a deep sauté pan, heat 3 cups of olive oil until it reaches 360 to

144

375 degrees. Take a large tablespoon, dipped in the remaining 1/4 cup olive oil, and scoop dough into hot olive oil 1 tablespoon at a time. Fill the bottom of the pan and cook dough until golden brown. Place cooked dough on a paper-towel-lined baking sheet. Continue process until all of the dough is used.

With a small knife, make a small hole in each piece of fried dough. Place the Pastry Cream in a small pastry bag with a round tip and fill the fried dough. When you are finished filling the bombolinis, roll each in powdered sugar. Serve at room temperature.

Makes 24.

Pastry Cream

2 cups whole milk
1/2 cup sugar
1/4 cup flour
5 egg yolks
1/2 teaspoon vanilla

In a small saucepan, combine the milk and sugar. Bring to a boil over medium heat. In a mixing bowl, combine flour, egg yolks and vanilla. Mix until smooth. Pour hot milk slowly into egg mixture and whisk into a smooth custard. Return the mixture to the saucepan. Over medium heat, cook the custard, stirring constantly with a wooden spoon, until it thickens. Pour the custard into a small pan and refrigerate until cool.

Makes about 2 cups.

Poached Pears with Honey Sauce
(Pere Con Salsa di Miele)

6 Bosc pears
3 cups cold water
1/2 vanilla bean
1 cup sugar
Juice of 1 large lemon
2 cups Honey Sauce

* * * * *

Peel and core the pears (a melon baller works well), leaving the stems intact. Place the cored pears in cold water and set aside. Mix 3 cups of water, the vanilla bean and the sugar in a saucepan large enough to hold all of the pears. Heat the syrup over medium heat until the sugar dissolves. Stir in the lemon juice. Drain the pears and add to the syrup. Cook over medium heat in covered pan, turning occasionally, until the pears are tender, about 30 minutes. Cool the pears in the syrup to room temperature, then refrigerate until cold. Remove the pears with a slotted spoon and place each pear on an individual dessert plate. Spoon the Honey Sauce over the pears.

Serves 6.

Honey Sauce

2 cups honey
Zest of 4 lemons
Zest of 4 oranges
1 teaspoon ground cloves
1 teaspoon cinnamon
1/2 teaspoon nutmeg

In a saucepan, heat the honey to a simmer over low heat. Add the lemon and orange zest, ground cloves, cinnamon and nutmeg. Mix well and cook over low heat for about 5 minutes. Serve warm or refrigerate to use later.

Prior to using the sauce, slowly reheat it to serve warm.

Makes 2 cups.

Ricotta Cheesecake

(Torta di Ricotta)

2 pounds fresh ricotta cheese

2/3 cup sugar

1/3 cup flour

4 eggs

1/2 teaspoon cinnamon

2 teaspoons vanilla

2 teaspoons orange zest

1/4 cup candied fruit

* * * * *

Preheat oven to 300 degrees. Butter and flour a 9-inch springform pan. In a large bowl, stir the cheese with a spatula until smooth. In another bowl, mix the sugar and flour. Stir mixture into the cheese until well blended. Add the eggs one at a time, mixing gently. Gently stir in the cinnamon, vanilla, orange zest and candied fruit.

Pour the mixture into the prepared pan and bake for about 1 hour and 15 minutes, or until lightly golden brown and almost firm in the center. Transfer the cake to a rack. When completely cold, cover with plastic wrap and refrigerate until serving time. Remove the sides of the pan and transfer to a platter for serving.

Serves 10 to 12.

Filled Holiday Crêpes
(Crespelle della Festa)

1/4 cup olive oil
Crêpe Batter
Crespelle Filling
Amaretto Sauce
1 cup powdered sugar

Crêpe Batter
1 cup flour
2 eggs
1 cup milk
3 tablespoons brandy
1/4 cup butter, melted and cooled to
    room temperature
3 ounces olive oil
1/2 teaspoon nutmeg
1/2 cup water

Crespelle Filling
1 medium apple, diced, with skin on,
    into 1/4-inch pieces
2 medium pears, diced, with skin

on, into 1/4-inch pieces
8 dry Mission figs, diced, with skin on,
    into 1/4-inch pieces
1/4 cup raisins
3 tablespoons brandy
2 tablespoons sugar
1/2 cup orange juice
Zest of 1 orange

Amaretto Sauce
1 cup amaretto
3/4 cup brown sugar
2 cups corn syrup
1/2 cup orange juice
1/4 cup cold water
2 tablespoons cornstarch

Begin by preparing the Crêpe Batter,
Crespelle Filling and Amaretto Sauce.

Crêpe Batter:

In a mixing bowl, combine all of the
    batter ingredients, stir thoroughly
    and set aside.

Crespelle Filling:

In a large mixing bowl, place the diced apple, pears and figs. Add the raisins, brandy, sugar, orange juice and orange zest. Mix well and cook in a saucepan over low heat until apples are tender, approximately 10 minutes. Cool to room temperature. Set aside.

Amaretto Sauce:

In a mixing bowl, combine the amaretto, brown sugar, corn syrup and orange juice. Place the mixture in a saucepan and bring to a boil. In the meantime, mix together the cold water and the cornstarch. Slowly add the cornstarch mixture to the amaretto mixture. Whisk together well. Reduce the heat and let the sauce simmer for about 10 minutes, or until ready to use.

Note: This sauce can be refrigerated and used at a later time. It can also be used warm or cold for a variety of different desserts.

To cook the crêpes:

Brush the bottom of a 6-inch nonstick sauté pan with some of the olive oil. Place the pan over high heat. Add 1/4 cup of batter and in a slow motion shake and tilt the pan so that the batter covers the bottom of the pan. Cook for approximately 1 minute, then turn to cook the other side. This will make a very thin crêpe that is light brown in color. Repeat the process until batter is gone. Set crêpes aside.

To fill the crêpes:

Lay 1 cooked crêpe on a flat surface, place 2 tablespoons of filling down the middle and roll like a sausage or a rope. Fill as many crêpes as you desire and set aside.

Lace the bottom of each dessert plate with warm Amaretto Sauce. Place a couple of the filled crêpes on top of the sauce and sprinkle with powered sugar.

Makes 24 to 36.

Neapolitan Cookies
(Taralle)

5 eggs, beaten
4 tablespoons butter, melted and cooled
1/2 cup sugar
1/4 cup milk
1/2 teaspoon vanilla
3 teaspoons baking powder
3 cups flour
1 cup powdered sugar
6 tablespoons water
1 teaspoon vanilla

* * * * *

Preheat oven to 375 degrees.
Place the beaten eggs in a large bowl or mixer. Add the melted butter and sugar gradually, stirring constantly with a wooden spoon. Add the milk, vanilla, baking powder and flour to make a firm but soft dough. Flour your hands, break off a small piece of dough and roll it into a thin 6-inch rope, approximately 1/2 inch in diameter. Shape the dough rope into a teardrop, joining the ends. Repeat with remaining dough.

Bake on a greased cookie sheet for approximately 15 minutes. Move cookies to a rack and cool.

For the icing, combine the powdered sugar, water and vanilla in a mixing bowl. Dip the cooled cookies into the icing and serve.

Makes 20 cookies.

"Taralle" are usually made for the holidays and are often dunked in espresso or cappuccino when eaten.

NOTES

NOTES

INDEX

FINITO

* * * * * * * * * * *

I hope you have enjoyed this journey
through the heritage of Buca di Beppo.
From Our Cucina to Your Kitchen.

The immigration continues...
Joseph P. Micatrotto

* * * * * * * * * * *